BARRON'S
HOW TO PREPARE FOR THE REGENTS COMPETENCY TEST IN WRITING

by Leon Gersten
Director of English
Deer Park Union Free School District, Deer Park, New York

BARRON'S EDUCATIONAL SERIES, INC.

© Copyright 1983 by Barron's Educational Series, Inc.

All rights reserved.
No part of this book may be reproduced in any form, by photostat, microfilm, xerography, or any other means, or incorporated into any information retrieval system, electronic or mechanical, without the written permission of the copyright owner.

All inquiries should be addressed to:
Barron's Educational Series, Inc.
250 Wireless Boulevard
Hauppauge, New York 11788

Library of Congress Catalog Card No. 82-13942
International Standard Book No. 0-8120-2381-1

Library of Congress Cataloging in Publication Data
Gersten, Leon.

 Barron's how to prepare for the Regents competency test in writing.

 Summary: Includes a diagnostic test, lessons, and model tests with sample answers to improve skills in writing business letters, reports, and persuasive compositions.
 1. English composition test. 2. High school equivalency examination. 3. English language—Composition and exercises. [1. English language—Composition and exercises—Ability testing—Study guides]
I. Barron's Educational Series, Inc. II. Title.
PE1408.G53 1982 808'.042'076 82-13942
ISBN 0-8120-2381-1

PRINTED IN THE UNITED STATES OF AMERICA
56789 100 987654

CONTENTS

INTRODUCTION   vi

    How This Book May Be Useful to You   vi
    How to Use This Book   vii

CHAPTER 1   The Regents Competency Test in Writing   1

    What Is the Regents Competency Test in Writing?   1
    How Are the Tests Rated?   2
    What Are Some General Guidelines You Should Know?   2
    Who Takes the Regents Competency Test in Writing?   2
    Why Is the Test Important?   3
    How Is the Test Used?   3
    What Are Some Useful Hints?   3
    How Can Your Writing Be Organized Effectively?   4
    Sample Exercises (with Sample Answers)   7

CHAPTER 2   A Diagnostic Test   12

    The Test   12
        Part I—Business Letter   12
        Part II—Report   13
        Part III—Composition   13
    Diagnosis: Model Papers   14

CHAPTER 3   Learning to Organize Your Ideas   26

    Pattern 1: Chronological Order   26
    Pattern 2: Ascending Order   28
    Pattern 3: Descending Order   30
    Pattern 4: Cause and Effect   31
    Pattern 5: Spatial Order   33
    Pattern 6: Comparison and Contrast   34

CHAPTER 4   Writing the Business Letter of Complaint   36

    Business Letter Checklist   38
    Thinking Through Problem Situations   39
        USING ASCENDING ORDER
    Lesson 1   Complaining about an Undeserved Traffic Ticket   41
    Lesson 2   Complaining about a Ticket Mixup   45
        USING DESCENDING ORDER
    Lesson 3   Complaining about a School Regulation   49
    Lesson 4   Complaining about Lost Baggage   53

Contents

USING CHRONOLOGICAL ORDER
Lesson 5   Complaining about a Lost Order — 57
Lesson 6   Complaining about a Misleading Ad — 61
Lesson 7   Complaining about an Inferior Product — 65
Lesson 8   Complaining about an Incident in a Restaurant — 69
Lesson 9   Complaining about an Inflated Bill — 73
Lesson 10 Complaining about an Unreceived Payment — 76
USING CAUSE AND EFFECT
Lesson 11 Complaining about a Teacher's Attitude — 80
Lesson 12 Complaining about an Unsatisfactory Travel Experience — 84

CHAPTER 5   Writing the Report — 88

Report Checklist — 89
Thinking Through Report Situations — 89
USING ASCENDING ORDER
Lesson 1   Reporting on a Talk by an Ex-Student — 91
Lesson 2   Reporting on an Interview with the School Principal — 95
USING DESCENDING ORDER
Lesson 3   Reporting on a Rally Against the Draft — 100
USING CHRONOLOGICAL ORDER
Lesson 4   Reporting on a Meeting with a Student Organization — 104
Lesson 5   Reporting on a School Event — 108
Lesson 6   Reporting on a School Board Meeting — 113
Lesson 7   Reporting on a Trip — 117
USING CAUSE AND EFFECT
Lesson 8   Reporting on Conditions in a Local Hospital — 121
USING COMPARISON
Lesson 9   Reporting on an Athletic Meet in Another School — 126
USING CONTRAST
Lesson 10 Reporting on a Friend's School Prom — 131
USING SPATIAL ORDER
Lesson 11 Reporting on a Live Television Program — 135
Lesson 12 Reporting on a Nature-Study Trip — 139

CHAPTER 6   Writing the Persuasive Composition — 144

Persuasive Composition Checklist — 145
Thinking Through Your Position and Reasons — 146
USING ASCENDING ORDER
Lesson 1   Persuading a School Principal to Drop a Subject from the Curriculum — 147
Lesson 2   Persuading a Teacher to Change a Mark — 151
Lesson 3   Persuading Readers of the School Paper about the Best Use for School Money — 155
Lesson 4   Persuading a Local Public Official That More Job Openings Are Needed — 159
USING DESCENDING ORDER
Lesson 5   Persuading the Town Council to Improve a Needed Service — 163
Lesson 6   Persuading the School Principal of the Need for a Smoking Room — 167

Contents

Lesson 7 Persuading Readers of the School Paper to Petition	171
USING CAUSE AND EFFECT	
Lesson 8 Persuading a TV Station to Upgrade Quality	175
Lesson 9 Persuading the Local Police to Patrol More Often	179
USING CHRONOLOGICAL ORDER	
Lesson 10 Persuading the Local School Board to Complete a Project	183
USING CONTRAST	
Lesson 11 Persuading a Legislator to Support Increased Funds for Schools	187
USING COMPARISON	
Lesson 12 Persuading Parents to Help Finance a Car	192

CHAPTER 7 Two Model Tests 197

Model Test 1	198
Part I—Business Letter	198
Part II—Report	199
Part III—Composition	200
Diagnosis: Model Papers	201
How to Evaluate Your Progress	206
Model Test 2	208
Part I—Business Letter	208
Part II—Report	209
Part III—Composition	209
Diagnosis: Model Papers	210
How to Evaluate Your Progress	214

GLOSSARY OF GRAMMATICAL TERMS 216

APPENDIX Basic Skills Review 217

Skill 1 Sentence Structure	218
Skill 2 Sentence Variety	228
Skill 3 Grammar and Syntax	232
Skill 4 Punctuation	234
Skill 5 Capitalization	238
Skill 6 Spelling and Usage	239
Answers	245

APPENDIX Answers for Chapter 3 246

INDEX 247

INTRODUCTION

HOW THIS BOOK MAY BE USEFUL TO YOU

This book is designed to prepare you for the Regents Competency Test in Writing. It will familiarize you with the types of compositions required and the processes involved in writing them successfully.

The book is organized into seven major chapters, three of which concentrate on the major tasks of the Regents Competency Test in Writing: the business letter, the report, and the persuasive composition. Each of these three chapters highlights the specific skills involved in completing a particular writing task successfully. Other chapters concentrate on the nature of the test and useful hints in preparing for it, the basic skill of learning to organize ideas logically, model tests to check progress, and a basic skills review to provide a brush-up in grammar and sentence structure.

Chapter 1 will introduce you to the test itself, with concrete samples to provide an understanding of what is required. Chapter 2, by means of a diagnostic test, will test your skills and provide model answers showing actual ability ranges; evaluations of each answer will give you insight on what you need to study further. Chapter 3 will teach you a key skill for any writing task: learning to organize your ideas effectively. Chapters 4, 5, and 6 each contain twelve lessons to reinforce one of the three writing tasks: business letter, report, and persuasive composition. Chapter 7 strengthens what you have learned by providing you with two model tests as well as sample answer papers to help diagnose your own progress. The Appendix provides a section on basic skills to help you write effectively, including skills in sentence structure and variety, grammar and usage, spelling, capitalization, and punctuation.

If you use this book wisely, you will gain in many ways. You will not only learn a variety of skills that will lead to more effective writing but you will also acquire a *process* of converting your thinking into smooth prose. That process will serve you well not just on the Regents Competency Test in Writing but in all writing situations. Process is simply a series of steps that lead to a quality product; in this case, competent writing.

Introduction

Writing is no mysterious art; it is a technique that can easily be learned from experience, practice, repetition, and a clear understanding of what is expected. This book, then, has one purpose: to sharpen your technique to the point where you can perform adequately in any writing situation.

HOW TO USE THIS BOOK

This book is organized to (1) familiarize you with the Regents Competency Test in Writing, (2) illustrate the three kinds of writing tasks you will be required to perform, (3) break these tasks into understandable components, and (4) show how to analyze a writing task and determine how to structure a piece of writing that is competent in both ideas and skills.

First, take the Diagnostic Test (*Chapter 2*) and analyze your own weaknesses. Once you have determined where you must place your attention, whether in organizing your ideas or in smoothing out sentence structure, etc., then go on to *Chapter 3*. Here you will learn how to organize your ideas effectively, using ascending or descending order, chronological order, comparison or contrast, spatial order, or cause and effect as a means to structure your writing.

Then go on to the three main chapters: *Chapter 4*—"Writing the Business Letter," *Chapter 5*—"Writing the Report," and *Chapter 6*—"Writing the Persuasive Composition." Each chapter includes twelve lessons. All thirty-six lessons follow a similar format. This is to help you recognize that writing a business letter, a report, or a persuasive composition requires a certain pattern.

Lesson Format

1. The Writing Task
2. Analysis of the Task
   What Are You Being Asked to Do?
   How to Respond
3. The Model
   Basic Components
   Evaluation
4. Follow-up Exercise
5. Final Analysis

Introduction

Within each lesson are developmental skills you should master before you actually write. Specifically, you should learn to follow a *process* of (1) reading a question and understanding how to respond to it, (2) setting up a preliminary outline, (3) expanding on that outline, (4) including components from good models in your own writing, and (5) evaluating and revising your finished product.

The models of good writing contained within each lesson are very important. You should study them for form, content, style, and organization. Note especially the marginal comments. These comments are keyed to the materials in the models. (For example, if transitionals are marked with a wavy line ~~~~ in the margin, then all transitionals in the model will also be marked with a wavy line.) Some key questions you should ask yourself as you read are:

**Checklist for Reading
Models of Good Writing**

1. What makes this an outstanding piece of writing?
2. How well does it carry out the prescribed task?
3. What are its outstanding features?
4. Which particular skills does it demonstrate?
5. How well organized is it?

These will help you, also, write more effectively.

When you have completed all lessons, go on to *Chapter 7* and take the two model tests. Be sure to analyze your weaknesses on Model Test 1 before continuing to Model Test 2.

Note that the "Basic Skills Review" in the *Appendix* should be referred to throughout your study of this book. It can serve as a reference to help you imitate the models of good writing or merely as a help in remedying your own writing weaknesses.

1
THE REGENTS COMPETENCY TEST IN WRITING

WHAT IS THE REGENTS COMPETENCY TEST IN WRITING?

The Regents Competency Test in Writing (RCT) is a test of your writing ability; it requires you to produce three separate pieces of written work: a business letter of complaint, a report based on information given, and a persuasive composition. Each topic for these tasks is presented in terms of a specific purpose and audience.

Each of the three tasks requires a piece of writing of about 100 to 200 words. For each, you are asked to prepare a first draft and then to edit and revise this before going on to your final work. Thus, you will be able to follow the process of planning, drafting, and revising.

HOW ARE THE TESTS RATED?

The method of rating is called *holistic*. This means that the three different pieces of writing you produce will be rated by different teachers and your final score will be the average of three part scores. Holistic evaluation helps to ensure a high degree of accuracy in the rating, since any one score on any one part of the test may not fairly reflect your true writing ability. In some schools, each piece of writing will be rated two or three times, depending on how many teachers are available.

WHAT ARE SOME GENERAL GUIDELINES YOU SHOULD KNOW?

There are certain qualities of good writing that the teachers who rate your paper will look for in your compositions. These raters will ask themselves questions such as the following:

1. Do you have a clear understanding of what you are to write?
2. Do you direct your writing to the proper audience?
3. Do you accomplish that writing task?
4. Do you use paragraphs to separate ideas?
5. Do you begin with an introductory idea and develop it consistently?
6. Do you connect your ideas well?
7. Are your details arranged logically and smoothly?
8. Are your sentences well-constructed?
9. Do you evidence a sound command of standard English?

These criteria will be the basis on which each of your compositions will be graded and will determine the mark you receive on each.

WHO TAKES THE REGENTS COMPETENCY TEST IN WRITING?

This test, commonly known as the RCT in Writing, is required of students in the eleventh grade who

1. Failed the Preliminary Regents Competency Test in Writing (PCT in Writing).

2. Scored below a certain level on a national test of skills.
3. Could not pass the Comprehensive Regents in English and therefore must pass a competency test.
4. Were identified by schools as generally deficient in basic writing skills.

WHY IS THE TEST IMPORTANT?

In some states, such as New York, the Regents Competency Test in Writing is a required measurement of a student's minimal writing skills. Passing this test, therefore, is one prerequisite for graduation for students who have already revealed consistent writing difficulties.

HOW IS THE TEST USED?

If you fail the Regents Competency Test in Writing, you will be given special help. Depending on the mark, this help will consist of individualized instruction in your regular English class, tutorial assistance, or placement in a special workshop class. The test mark will be used to measure whether you need general or intensive follow-up to improve your writing skills. You may take the test as often as necessary until you pass.

WHAT ARE SOME USEFUL HINTS?

First and foremost, get a good night's sleep so that you can come to the exam with a clear mind. Prime yourself to achieve this goal of writing: carefully thought-out ideas that represent the best model of how you think on a subject. Remember, good thinking generates effective writing.

When you receive your test paper, take the time to read each task completely—several times if necessary. The key here is complete understanding of what the task you are to perform requires. Underline key words and parts of the test to highlight the direction you are to take and to remind you to keep to that direction.

The very best beginning is a preliminary outline to pave the way for the final product. Study your outline carefully to see whether it fulfills the task to be performed. Rearrange, shift, and cross out where necessary to refine your outline. It is a good idea at this point to reread the directions to be sure you are on the right track.

Use the refined outline to write your first draft. Examine this draft to see that it satisfies the directions, contains all the given information, and is suitably paragraphed.

- *If it is a business letter of complaint*, be sure it contains all the facts.
- *If it is a report*, be sure it contains all the details provided and arranges those details in the appropriate order.
- *If it is a persuasive paper*, be sure it states a position clearly and supports it with convincing reasons.

In all cases, check to see that you have begun with a clear statement of purpose, developed that purpose, and concluded with a rephrasing of that purpose.

Use your best handwriting to enhance clarity.

HOW CAN YOUR WRITING BE ORGANIZED EFFECTIVELY?

There are many ways to arrange your ideas in writing, and how you arrange them is most important in fulfilling the task. The choice of arrangement you make, therefore, will enable you to be clearer and more effective in all three types of writing: the Business Letter of Complaint, the Report, and the Persuasive Composition.

The following are possible patterns you can use to fit the purpose of your writing task.

Chronological Order

Arrange details as they actually happened.

Example

I barely recall what happened during the accident. First, I saw the fire rage through a window. Second, I remember running into the burning building. Third, I grabbed the woman by the arm and helped her out the door.

Descending Order

Arrange reasons or details from the *most important one* to the second and third *less important ones*.

Example

Old people in our society need our recognition and respect. <u>Most important, they are human beings who, in spite of their age, have feelings.</u> Also, they have worked, raised families, and contributed fully. Finally, they can still make many important contributions to society and to the quality of life of those who seek to know them.

Ascending Order

Arrange details and reasons from *less important to the most important*.

Example

There was much excitement at the local Democratic meeting. A crowd of members pushed into the meeting hall. Later, there was a loud discussion of the primary issue. <u>But the most dramatic occurrence was a fight between two speakers.</u> What an exciting night!

Cause and Effect

Arrange ideas so that a relationship between an influence and an outcome is shown.

Example

```
                              23 Cherry Lane
                              Akron, Ohio 19067
                              December 5, 1982

Jay's Restaurant
156 Greene Avenue
Akron, Ohio 19067

Dear Manager:

   I am writing to complain about your
policy with regard to smoking. Because        The cause
you do not have a "no smoking" section,
I suffered a great deal while eating.

   The smoke interfered with my
appetite, made the room stuffy, and           The effects
caused an allergic reaction that
continued to the next day.
```

> Dining and smoking just do not mix.
> Therefore you certainly should separate
> smokers from nonsmokers.
>
> >Complainingly yours,
> >*Jerome Kramer*
> >Jerome Kramer

Comparison

Show either similarities or dissimilarities.

Example

Paris is a teeming city, like New York. Its Louvre Museum compares favorably with the Metropolitan Museum of Art in Manhattan. The Eiffel Tower, which is spectacular, matches the size of the Empire State Building. In many other ways, such as its streets, population, and department stores, the city of Paris is reminiscent of New York.

The city of Paris is seen as very similar to New York

Contrast

Show distinct differences, obvious dissimilarities.

Example

My observations of the Athletic League showed how different it was from the Boy Scouts. The League meeting started promptly, had an agenda, and proceeded with a clear purpose, unlike the free-for-all atmosphere of the Boy Scout troop session. League members were really interested and involved in plans for activities, while the Scouts just went through the motions. Clearly, the Athletic League has many more advantages for its members than does the Boy Scout organization.

The Athletic League is shown to be superior to the Boy Scouts

Spatial Order

Arrange details of a physical setting in an orderly pattern, such as describing objects in a room from left to right, from near to far, etc.

Example

The waiting-room of the railroad had an eerie quality. The benches were long and narrow, like long arms reaching into the night. The gates to the tracks creaked and sent chills down my spine. Other passengers were bent over like snapped twigs. The gray light overhead was like a flashlight in a completely dark room.

The writer observes the surrounding physical details and describes them

SAMPLE EXERCISES

The following sample exercises are presented to give you an overview of the three major writing tasks you will confront on the Regents Competency Test in Writing. They serve as a preview of later chapters and lessons, which follow a similar pattern of skill- and-content development.

These sample exercises should be used to increase skills in (1) fulfilling the writing task on the basis of the directions given, (2) thinking and expressing ideas, (3) planning and outlining the final product, (4) understanding the merits of superior writing, (5) evaluating your own writing, and (6) analyzing for completeness and accuracy.

Part I—Business Letter

Directions

Use the proper business-letter form in responding to the situation below.

On May 5, you sent a check for $55 to Columbia Electronics for a tape recorder, Catalog No. 143. On June 3, you received a tape recorder, Catalog No. 155, which does not have the features you wanted.

Write a letter of complaint to this address: Columbia Electronics, 45 Listen Boulevard, Chicago, Illinois 60622.

When you write your letter, remember to:

- *Fulfill the situation above.*
- *Offer a solution.*
- *Follow the format of a proper business letter.*

The Regents Competency Test in Writing

Part II—Report

Directions

The report you write should be based on the details below. Before you begin to write, arrange these details in proper order.

The president of your student council has asked you to interview a French student who now goes to your school. You are to write a report for the council members. The following details are what you recorded when you interviewed him.

> Henri Berg from Bordeaux, France
> Sends letters to his family in France
> Visited New Orleans for the Mardi Gras
> "My dream is to live in the U.S."
> Takes notes on all his trips
> Stays with a host family in New York
> Loves pizza and Big Macs
> "I enjoy being with American teenagers."
> Compares American high schools to the French lycée
> Plans to go to college in the U.S.
> Enjoys cross-country bicycling
> Has a good command of English
> Is popular with teachers and fellow students

Arrange these notes in proper order. Then write a report that includes all the information in the notes.

Part III—Composition

Directions

Write an essay in which you try to convince your local assemblyman that your opinion on the topic described below is sound.

The state assembly has proposed a bill which permits students to quit school at the age of fifteen. Determine your position on the legal age of quitting school.

Write an essay of about 200 words stating your position and giving at least two convincing reasons to support that position.

SAMPLE ANSWERS

Part I—Business Letter

Heading
12 Downing Street
Buffalo, New York 43169
June 5, 1983

Inside address
Columbia Electronics
45 Listen Boulevard
Chicago, Illinois 60622

Salutation
Dear Sirs:

   I wish to bring attention to an error on your part. On May 5, I ordered a tape recorder, Catalog No. 143, costing $55, but received, instead, tape recorder, Catalog No. 155, on June 3.

PARAGRAPH 1: *States the purpose of the letter*

   I was planning to use this tape recorder on a camping trip. However, the tape recorder you sent, Catalog No. 155, does not have the range of features that I wanted. It cannot serve my purpose. As a result, I feel that I have been severely inconvenienced.

PARAGRAPH 2: *Supports the purpose with facts and other information (chronological order)*

   Please rectify this error by replacing tape recorder, Catalog No. 155, which is being returned under separate cover, with the tape recorder originally ordered, Catalog No. 143. I hope you will attend to this matter immediately.

PARAGRAPH 3: *States what the writer expects as an outcome*

Sincerely yours,

Leonard Jones

Leonard Jones

Complimentary close

Signature

Analysis

The above letter is generally well done and would receive a high score. It satisfies the following criteria:

1. It explains the problem.
2. It explains what the writer wants the company to do.
3. It gives complete and correct information.
4. It uses an acceptable business letter form.

Part II—Report

Henri Berg, a visiting student from France, is now living with a host family in New York while attending our high school. Since he misses his family, he sends letters home frequently. His future plan, after returning home, is to go to college in the United States.

PARAGRAPH 1: *Groups details around the student's overall plans*

In addition to going to school, Henri Berg travels a great deal. While visiting famous places, such as New Orleans during the Mardi Gras, he takes a lot of notes. His notes include observations about American youth. He has said, "I enjoy being with American teenagers." With regard to this country, he has also said, "My dream is to live in the United States some day."

PARAGRAPH 2: *Groups details around trips and general impressions (comparison and contrast)*

Since Henri has a good command of English, he is popular with his teachers and fellow students. Often, they get together to enjoy cross-country bicycling, as well as to eat pizza and Big Macs. He compares American high schools favorably to the French lycée he has attended in Bordeaux.

PARAGRAPH 3: *Groups details around the student's ability to relate to others*

Analysis

The above report is generally good and would receive a high score. It satisfies the following criteria:

1. All the details are used.
2. The details are arranged according to three main categories.
3. Paragraphs are used to separate these three categories.
4. The details are organized logically.
5. The report fulfills the assigned writing task.

The Regents Competency Test in Writing

Part III—Composition

I strongly oppose the bill in our state assembly that would allow young people to leave school at age fifteen. Passage of such a bill would do more harm than good. *PARAGRAPH 1: writer's position on the issue*

My most important reason for opposing this bill is that teenagers leaving school at such an early age would be poorly prepared for employment. Considering the number of people now without jobs, what chance would a fifteen-year-old have in competition with older people? *PARAGRAPH 2: most important reason first (descending order of importance)*

Secondly, leaving school at an early age is no alternative to a sound education. The purpose of high school is to teach those skills necessary for a successful career. Without minimal competency in reading, writing, and mathematics, as well as a high-school diploma, a young person will be bidding unsuccessfully for a job with more educated people. *PARAGRAPH 3: second important reason*

Finally, a fifteen-year-old, regardless of the reason, is immature. Time is needed to develop a sense of independence, resourcefulness, and direction. Remaining in school, at least until the age of seventeen, allows teenagers a necessary developmental phase. *PARAGRAPH 4: third important reason*

For these reasons, I urge you to do your utmost to defeat the bill permitting young people to leave school at age fifteen. *PARAGRAPH 5: restatement of the opening position*

Analysis

The above composition is a good one and would receive a high score. It satisfies the following criteria:

1. The first paragraph states the writer's position.
2. The reasons for this position are given clearly.
3. The reasons are organized according to an order of importance (descending order).
4. The last paragraph re-emphasizes the writer's position.
5. The entire composition makes a convincing argument.

2

A DIAGNOSTIC TEST

THE TEST

Part I—Business Letter

Directions

Use the proper business-letter form in responding to the situation below.

Early in October, you saw a newspaper ad placed by the Exeter Book Company for *Famous Movie Stars*. On October 8, you sent off a $9.89 check for a copy of this book. On November 5, you received a book called *Oscar Winners*.

Write a business letter outlining your problem to Exeter Book Company, Inc., 1109 Broad Hollow Road, Newton, NY 10521.

When you write your letter, remember to:

- *Fulfill the situation above.*
- *Offer a solution.*
- *Follow the format of a proper business letter.*

A Diagnostic Test

Part II—Report

Directions

The report you write should be based on the details below. Before you begin to write, arrange these details in proper order.

Your social studies class is studying prison conditions. You attended a meeting at which ex-convicts spoke about their experiences in prison. Your teacher has asked you to write a report of the meeting for your class. The notes you took at the meeting are shown in the accompanying box.

> Date: May 5
> Speakers: Bob Smith, Andrew Kline, ex-convicts
> Prison rehabilitation doesn't seem to work
> Guards are cruel and exploitative
> Cells are bare and depressing
> Meeting conducted in a church classroom
> "I learned nothing useful in Attica," says Andrew Kline
> "You have to learn the ropes or you perish," comments Bob Smith
> The cost of keeping a man in prison for life is astronomical
> Many prisoners become apathetic and lose faith in society
> Prisoners soon learn how to get around regulations
> There are agencies to help the ex-offender
> Former inmates can call a hotline
> Many men get sick and receive poor medical care

Arrange these notes in proper order. Then write a report that includes all the information in the notes.

Part III—Composition

Directions

Write an essay in which you try to convince your friends that your opinion on the topic described on the next page is sound.

A Diagnostic Test

You have read a newspaper article suggesting that young men 18 and older may be drafted into the service. You have given this possibility a great deal of thought and have come up with a position you feel is defensible. However, your friends hold different opinions.

Write a composition of at least 200 words explaining to your friends your position on the draft and why you hold it. Give two reasons. Explain each reason.

DIAGNOSIS: MODEL PAPERS
Part I—Business Letter

Student A: Poor

October 8, 1982

Incomplete heading

Exeter Book Company, Inc

Incomplete inside address

Dear Sirs,

Use a colon

You made a mistake on my order, you sent me the wrong book for the money I sent you. How can you make such a mistake, I'm really annoyed, when I want the book so much. So I'm returning the book for the write one.

Poor organization of details

Lack of clarity

Faulty sentence structure

Sheila Adams

Needs a complimentary close

Diagnosis

On the basis of 100 points, this letter might get 50, for the following reasons:

1. The student explains the problem but does not include the details given in the assignment.
2. The student explains what she wants the company to do but does not clarify her expectations.

A Diagnostic Test

3. The student does not give complete information.
4. The student does not use an acceptable business letter form.
5. The student is weak in basic skills. For example:

   Error 1: You made a mistake on my order, you sent me the wrong book for the money I sent you.
   Correction: You made a mistake on my order by sending me the wrong book.

   Error 2: How can you make such a mistake, I'm really annoyed, when I want the book so much.
   Correction: How can you make such a mistake? I'm really annoyed, since I want the book so much.

   Error 3: So Im returning the book for the write one.
   Correction: Therefore, I'm returning the book for the right one.

Student B: Fair

> 20 Nancy Lane
> Nesconset, New York

Incomplete heading—needs a date and a zip code

> Exeter Book Company
> 1109 Broad Hollow Road
> Newton, New York

Incomplete inside address—needs a zip code

> Dear Sirs:
>
> I wish to tell you that I received the wrong book for the check I sent in. It was obviously an error on your part, because I got a book about Oscar winners instead of one on famous movie stars.
>
> Please forward the correct book.
>
> Truly Yours
> Bob Vincent

Does not include specifics—name of book, price

Incorrect complimentary close

A Diagnostic Test

Diagnosis

On the basis of 100 points, this letter might get 75, for the following reasons:

1. The student is not specific enough in giving the details of his problem.
2. The student does not use an acceptable business letter form.
3. The student does not flesh out the second paragraph.
4. The student shows a fair command of basic skills.

Student C: Excellent

14 Fairway Avenue
Troy, NY 16740
November 7, 1982

— Acceptable heading

Acceptable inside address —

Exeter Book Company, Inc.
1109 Broad Hollow Road
Newton, NY 10521

Salutation —

Dear Sirs:

I am distressed over the error you made in my book order. On October 8, I sent you a check for $9.89 for Famous Movie Stars, but received instead, on November 5, Oscar Winners.

— Clear statement of purpose of letter—good use of details (chronological order)

Since I sent for this book a long time ago, expecting to use it as a reference, I am naturally disappointed. Therefore, I am returning Oscar Winners so that you can ship Famous Movie Stars immediately.

— Good use of sentence structure. Expression of disappointment

Very truly yours,

Jerry Lundigan

— Acceptable complimentary close

A Diagnostic Test

Diagnosis

On the basis of 100 points, the above letter might receive 100, a perfect score, for the following reasons:

1. The problem is fully explained.
2. All the given details are used.
3. The student makes clear exactly what he expects.
4. A variety of well-constructed sentences is used.
5. An acceptable business letter form is used.

NOTE: Success on this part of the test, the business letter of complaint, depends on both competency and correctness. "Competency" refers to developing and expressing your message in a full, logical, and coherent manner, while "correctness" refers to the proper use of language and the components of the business letter form.

Part II—Report

Student A: Poor

Lack of paragraphing

Omission of many of the notes given

> The meeting with prisoners was great. You see, we met with them in a room and listened to them tell us about conditions. Which are very bad. Some talked alot. Mostly about regulations and cruel guards, and depressing cells. One guy said I learned nothing useful in Attica, and another guy said you have to learn the ropes or you perish. Its pretty bad to be in prison, prison rehabilitation doesn't work.

Poor organization of notes

No clear sequencing of detail

Poorly constructed sentences

Diagnosis

On the basis of 100 points, this report might get 40, for the following reasons:

1. The student has not organized the notes into any clear pattern.
2. The student omits some of the given information.
3. The student has not structured his writing into paragraphs to show unit ideas.
4. The student does not have a clear sense of the writing task.
5. The student has a poor command of basic skills, for example:

Error 1: You see, we met with them in a room and listened to them tell us about conditions.
Correction: We met with them in a church classroom and listened to them tell us about conditions.

Error 2: Which was very bad.
Correction: The conditions were very bad.

Error 3: Some talked alot. Mostly about regulations and cruel guards, and depressing cells.
Correction: Some talked a lot, mostly about regulations, cruel guards, and depressing cells.

Error 4: One guy said I learned nothing useful in Attica, and another guy said you have to learn the ropes or you perish.
Correction: One inmate said, "I learned nothing useful in Attica," while another remarked, "You have to learn the ropes or you perish."

Error 5: Its pretty bad to be in prison, prison rehabilitation doesn't work.
Correction: It's pretty bad to be in prison, and prison rehabilitation doesn't work.

A Diagnostic Test

Student B: Good

I went to a meeting on May 5 to hear two ex-convicts speak about prison conditions. According to what they both had to say, generally speaking, prison rehabilitation doesn't seem to be working. Guards are cruel and exploitative, cells are bare and depressing, many men get sick and receive poor medical care, and many prisoners become apathetic and lose faith in society.

Prisoners soon learn how to get around regulations. "You have to learn the ropes or you perish," comments Bob Smith. "I learned nothing useful in Attica," says Andrew Kline. The cost of keeping a man in prison for life is astronomical, it seems.

During the meeting, held in a church classroom, it was pointed out that there are agencies to help ex-offenders as well as a hot-line that former inmates can call.

PARAGRAPH 1: Purpose of the meeting

Details to support the purpose

PARAGRAPH 2: The need to survive in prison in the face of impossible odds

PARAGRAPH 3: Where the meeting was held and practical advice given

Diagnosis

On the basis of 100 points, this report might get 80, for the following reasons:

1. The student has a sense of organization.
2. The student has arranged the notes in logical order, showing that he or she has a fairly good idea of what happened at the meeting.
3. The student uses paragraphs to set off groups of ideas.
4. The student employs various sentence structures that help to keep the reader's attention.
5. The student has a sound command of basic skills.

Student C: Excellent

On May 5, I attended a meeting on prison conditions which was held in a nearby church classroom. There, two ex-convicts spoke at length on prisons today and the treatment of inmates. The speakers, Bob Smith and Andrew Kline, told of their first-hand experience and described the conditions that work against rehabilitation.

According to both speakers, prisoners tend to become apathetic and lose faith in society for several reasons: guards are sometimes cruel and exploitative, cells are bare and depressing, and many of those who become ill receive poor medical care. These and other conditions make the prisoners feel resentful. Often inmates live for only one reason: survival. Andrew Kline put it this way: "I learned nothing useful in Attica," meaning that he was merely confined and not taught any useful skills. Bob Smith made it clear that survival is the key. "You have to learn the ropes or you perish," he added.

Although little is being done to prepare prisoners to make their way back into society as useful citizens, a lot is being done for the ex-offender. According to the speakers, there are agencies that offer help to job seekers. There is also a hot-line that ex-convicts can use at any time to get support or advice in emergencies.

PARAGRAPH 1: Where and when the meeting took place

Purpose of the meeting

The speakers and what they spoke about

PARAGRAPH 2: Attitudes of inmates and reasons why such attitudes develop (descending order)

Testimony of the speakers

PARAGRAPH 3: Helping ex-inmates adjust to society

> *After the meeting, I went home with a better sense of what prisons are like. I felt that if our penal system is to rehabilitate criminals, a great deal will have to change before this goal can be achieved.*

PARAGRAPH 4: Writer's own conclusion based on the facts

Diagnosis

This report, on the basis of 100 points, might receive a full 100, for the following reasons:

1. The student has organized the notes into a final report that is both interesting and informative.
2. The student has arranged the notes into a pattern of *descending order*. He or she first develops the primary theme of deplorable prison conditions and their effect on inmates, then deals with the resulting attitudes about survival, and finally shows that change is necessary before real progress can be made.
3. The student develops each idea in a separate paragraph, and each follows smoothly from the one before.
4. The student expands fully on the notes given.
5. The student has excellent basic skills as well as a good grasp of sentence structure, syntax, and organization.

NOTE: Success on this part of the test, the report, depends in large measure on how well you arrange the notes. Depending on the situation, the arrangement can be (1) chronological, (2) in terms of contrast/comparison, (3) spatial, (4) according to cause and effect, (5) in descending order of importance, or (6) in ascending order of importance. The key is to study the notes you are given so as to determine which pattern will convey the information most accurately and completely in your written report.

A Diagnostic Test

Part III—Composition

Student A: Poor

The idea of a draft for 18-year-olds is stupid. Nonsense. Out of the question. That's my opinion, to say the least. How can they think of drafting young people and sending them to war? It doesn't make sense, these legislators are so stupid. Besides, 18-year-olds are not mature enough, anyone knows that.

What the country should do is have a volunteer sign-up law, so young men can join up for money or career. That way, students wanting an education don't have to serve and interrupt there schooling. It really makes more sense to do it that way. I say no draft law for young people unless they choose to join the military.

PARAGRAPH 1: Has no clear direction; Too wordy, without saying anything important; Poor sentence structure

PARAGRAPH 2: Poorly supported argument; unclear reasoning

Ineffective conclusion

Diagnosis

On the basis of 100 points, this composition might get 50, for the following reasons:

1. The student's position is not clearly defined.
2. The student's reasons for holding that position are therefore weak.
3. The student has not organized his or her writing effectively.
4. The student does not show logical thinking.
5. The student has not used paragraphs to develop separate ideas.
6. The student uses poor sentence structure throughout.
7. The student has a weak command of basic skills, for example:
   Error 1: The idea of a draft for 18-year olds is stupid. Nonsense. Out of the question.
   Correction: The idea of a draft for 18-year-olds is stupid, nonsensical, and out of the question.

A Diagnostic Test

Error 2: It doesn't make sense, these legislators are so stupid.
Correction: It doesn't make sense; these legislators are so narrow in their thinking.
Error 3: Besides, 18-year-olds are not mature enough, anyone knows that.
Correction: Anyone knows that 18-year-olds are not mature enough.
Error 4: there schooling
Correction: their schooling

Student B: Fair

> The recent proposal by Congress that a law be enacted drafting 18-year-olds into the armed forces is, in my opinion, a good idea. We as a nation must have young people who are ready to defend us in times of crisis. Besides, any person born in this country, enjoying all our liberties, should be proud to serve his country. Since there are world situations that may lead to war, like Iran and Afghanistan, we should be ready for an unexpected attack. Only by building a strong army and having it ready for defense will we be able to preserve our freedoms. Young people, therefore, should accept this responsibility willingly. I personally will be happy to be drafted to serve this country.

Annotations:
- Writer's position
- Reason 1—needs a separate paragraph
- Reason 2—needs a separate paragraph
- Reason 3—needs a separate paragraph
- Conclusion needs a separate paragraph

Diagnosis

On the basis of 100 points, this composition might get 75, for the following reasons:

1. The student states his or her position but does not support it with convincing reasons.
2. The student does not organize his or her ideas into separate paragraphs.

A Diagnostic Test

3. The student has not arranged his or her details in any logical pattern.
4. The student has been too brief.
5. The student has a fairly good command of basic skills.

Student C: Excellent

I am strongly in favor of the proposed draft law to have 18-year-olds serve for two years. Considering the pros and cons of the issue, I see no other way that we, as a nation, can protect ourselves from the dangers that exist.

    First, nations like China and Russia are building their military strength to a capacity that threatens our peace and security. To allow ourselves to fall behind militarily would be to open our door to the invaders. We should arm in order to be strong.

    Second, since the unemployment rate for the young is the highest ever, serving in the army would allow our young men to make decisions about their lives and to acquire skills that would serve them well later on. Instead of wasting their time, young people can provide a needed service as well as gain better insight into their future goals.

    Third and most important, our youth have a responsibility to join in the defense of this nation when it is in danger. In no other nation in the world do people enjoy such freedom and democracy as we do. We therefore owe our government, and its citizens, allegiance at all times.

PARAGRAPH 1: Writer's position stated clearly and fleshed out

PARAGRAPH 2: Reason 1—the threat of invasion and what to do about it

PARAGRAPH 3: Reason 2—the opportunity to learn skills to create a better future

PARAGRAPH 4: Reason 3—what we owe this nation—a responsibility everyone has—the most important reason (ascending order)

> *For the above reasons, I strongly support the draft law as a necessary security measure. Without it, we would be open to attack, and all that we stand for would go down the drain. Any person who is proud of this great country would agree.*

PARAGRAPH 5: Concluding statement reemphasizing the opening position

Diagnosis

On the basis of 100 points, this composition might get 95, for the following reasons:

1. The student has a clear, defined position that is plainly stated and that he adheres to throughout.
2. The student supports that position with three strong reasons.
3. The student has arranged the reasons according to an ascending pattern (first reason, second reason, and, finally, third and most important reason).
4. The student has organized the composition logically and coherently.
5. The student uses paragraphs to separate one idea from another.
6. The student has an excellent command of basic skills.

NOTE: Success on this part of the test, the persuasive composition, depends largely on how you arrange and organize your reasons. Depending on the position and the issue, the arrangement can be (1) in ascending order, (2) in descending order, (3) in chronological order, (4) according to cause and effect, (5) in terms of comparison/contrast, or (6) in spatial order. The key to a good grade is to think through your position first, state it clearly and directly, outline your supporting reasons, and then determine which arrangement works best to convey your position on the issue.

3

LEARNING TO ORGANIZE YOUR IDEAS

Since the Regents Competency Test in Writing requires that you organize your ideas in a logical and coherent manner, knowing the variety of organizational patterns is essential.

PATTERN 1: CHRONOLOGICAL ORDER

Chronological means time order. This is the most common pattern in all three writing tasks: the business letter, the report, and the persuasive composition. This pattern includes: What happened first, what happened second, what happened next, etc.

Here is an example of a report written by a student. Can you judge why it is poorly organized?

Example

The Student Athletic League ended too late. I got home at almost midnight. Our president had asked for more support for

Learning to Organize Your Ideas

team activities. When the meeting began at 8 P.M., we discussed membership dues. Before that, we had assembled outside in the street.

Analysis The above report is poorly organized because the details of the meeting are not in proper time order (chronological). The details should be rearranged, as follows:

What happened *first:*	Before the meeting began, we assembled outside in the street.
What happened *second:*	When the meeting began at 8 P.M., we discussed membership dues.
What happened *next:*	Later, our president asked for more support for team activities.
What happened *last:*	The Student Athletic League ended too late. I got home at almost midnight.

Now put it all together as a paragraph, one in which the details are in chronological order.

Reconstructed Paragraph

Before the meeting began, we assembled outside in the street. When the meeting began, at 8 P.M., we discussed membership dues. Later, our president asked for more support for team activities. The Student Athletic League ended too late. I got home at almost midnight.

Test (See answers on page 246.)

Directions

Now see whether you understand chronological order, by rearranging the following details and constructing a paragraph.

Detail 1: Our second speaker at the Youth Rehabilitation Center asked for our support.

Detail 2: The last item on the agenda was the matter of volunteering time.

Detail 3: Before that, there was a plea by the treasurer for dues payment.
Detail 4: The first speaker was an ex-offender who spoke about his life.
Detail 5: The meeting started early and ended early.

PATTERN 2: ASCENDING ORDER

This pattern of arranging your ideas reserves the most important detail for last. All the details are arranged in this manner: One important reason, another important reason, the *most important reason*. It's like saving the knock-out punch for last.

Here is an example of a business letter written by a student. Can you judge why it is not in ascending order?

Example

>4 Mary Lane
>Knowles, Idaho 45430
>January 15, 1983

Jersey Athletic Club
1343 North Avenue
Boise, Idaho 45434

Dear Mr. Langley:

   My most important reason for writing is to tell you that I sent in $10 for a membership card two months ago, but haven't received it yet. I'm annoyed, too, at the delay. Also, I've heard so much about your club and am therefore disappointed. Please send the card quickly.

>Sincerely yours,
>
>*Elayne Gerst*
>
>Elayne Gerst

Learn to Organize Your Ideas

Analysis The above letter is poorly organized because the details are not properly arranged in ascending order. The details should be arranged as follows:

One important reason:	I'm annoyed at the delay.
Another important reason:	I've heard so much about your club and am therefore disappointed.
The *most important* reason:	I sent in $10 for a membership card two months ago, but haven't received it yet.

Now put it all together in ascending order, and you have the following improved paragraph.

Reconstructed Letter

```
                              4 Mary Lane
                              Knowles, Idaho 45430
                              January 15, 1983

Jersey Athletic Club
1343 North Avenue
Boise, Idaho 45434

Dear Mr. Langley:

   I'm writing to tell you I'm annoyed
at the delay in receiving my membership
card. I've heard so much about your
club and am therefore disappointed.
Most important, I sent in $10 for a
membership card two months ago, but
haven't received it yet. Please send
the card quickly.

                         Sincerely yours,
                         Elayne Gerst
                         Elayne Gerst
```

Learning to Organize Your Ideas

Test (See answers on page 246.)

Directions

Now see whether you understand the pattern of ascending order by rearranging the following details on an insurance claim in which the insured is still waiting for the settlement.

Detail 1: One important reason is that it's a hardship to wait and wait.

Detail 2: The most important reason is that I can't fix the car till I receive a settlement.

Detail 3: Another important reason is that your agent already checked the damage and filed the claim.

PATTERN 3: DESCENDING ORDER

This pattern of arranging your ideas gives the most important detail first. All the details are arranged in this manner: The most important reason, another important reason, a third important reason.

Here is an example of a persuasive paper written by a student. Can you judge why it is not in descending order?

Example

Running for political office is motivated by a number of reasons. A candidate has to have a generous desire to help others. Most of all, a person who wants to get elected must have the ability to make changes in society. He or she should be concerned about the problems people face. Since it is a challenging job, only the best candidates should strive for political office.

Analysis The above persuasive paragraph lists three reasons for running for office, but not in proper descending order sequence. The most important detail should be written first, as follows:

The *most important* reason:	A person who wants to get elected must have the ability to make changes in society.
Another important reason:	A candidate has to have a generous desire to help others.
A *third* important reason:	He or she should be concerned about the problems people face.

Now put it all together in descending order and you have the following improved paragraph.

Reconstructed Paragraph

Running for political office is motivated by a number of reasons. Most of all, a person who wants to get elected must have the ability to make changes in society. Another important quality for a person who wants to get elected is a generous desire to help others. Thirdly, he or she should be concerned about the problems people face. Since it is a challenging job, only the best candidates should strive for political office.

Test (See answers on page 246.)

Directions

Now see whether you understand the pattern of descending order by rearranging the following qualities.

Quality 1: It's also important for a father to play with his children.
Quality 2: Above all, a father should be very understanding and sympathetic.
Quality 3: A father should take interest in his children.

After you have rearranged the above qualities, write a paragraph in which these qualities reflect a father's role in the family.

PATTERN 4: CAUSE AND EFFECT

This pattern of arranging your ideas shows a relationship between one event (cause) that results in another event (effect).

In the following report, can you identify the cause and effect events?

Example

World War II was a complex result of a number of contributing causes. Nazi Germany's expanding territorial needs led them to invade such nations as Poland and Belgium. The memory

Learning to Organize Your Ideas

of defeat in World War I created a revengeful attitude toward England and France. The growth of Germany's industry justified the conquest of rich natural resources in Alsace–Lorraine. These seeds of emerging totalitarianism germinated into a period of bloodshed and destruction.

Analysis   The above report on the growth of Nazi Germany lists three primary causes that led to the war itself. The relationship is as follows:

Cause: Nazi Germany's expanding territorial needs
Effect: led them to invade such nations as Poland and Belgium.

Cause: The memory of defeat in World War I
Effect: created a revengeful attitude toward England and France.

Cause: The growth of Germany's industry
Effect: justified the conquest of rich natural resources in Alsace–Lorraine.

REMEMBER: A cause-and-effect relationship shows how one event leads to another.

Test (See answers on page 246.)

Directions

Study the following notes for a report on school vandalism. Arrange them in a cause-and-effect order. Then write a full report containing this information.

NOTES

Frequent break-ins in schools
Costs of repairs are high
Custodians have to deal with intruders
The taxpayers bear the burden of loss
Students are usually the perpetrators
They show their disregard for property
Other maintenance is being ignored
There is a lot of damage to windows

Learning to Organize Your Ideas

PATTERN 5: SPATIAL ORDER

Spatial is an adjective derived from the noun *space*. It refers to any physical area in which objects or people can be seen. *This pattern, then, includes all the observable details within a particular area.*

In the following paragraph, can you identify all the spatial details observed by the writer?

Example

> *I visited the Lion House in the zoo to become acquainted with the king of the beasts. While there, I noticed the thick steel bars that separate lions from people. The lighting from the side of the wall is dim so as not to blind the creatures. A food trough contains chunks of meat brought by an attendant three times a day. Water streams into the cage by means of a hose attached to the outside.*

Analysis The above report contains what the visitor to the zoo sees inside the lion's cage. The spatial details are:

- Thick steel bars that separate lions from people
- Lighting from the side of the wall that is dim so that the creatures are not blinded
- A food trough that contains chunks of meat
- Water that streams into the cage by means of a hose attached to the outside

REMEMBER: Spatial details need not be only visual; they can be smells, sounds, sensations.

Test (See answers on page 246.)

Directions

Study the following spatial details observed in a supermarket. Rearrange them in any order that captures the feeling of a supermarket. Then write a paragraph in which these spatial details are used.

- Long aisles that lead to food sections
- Noisy, busy stream of people
- A variety of aromas that permeates the store
- Cashiers busily ringing registers
- Food shelves stocked plentifully

Learning to Organize Your Ideas

Now think of a simpler situation: your own room. List three major spatial details of the room. Then write a paragraph describing this room.

Spatial detail 1: _____

Spatial detail 2: _____

Spatial detail 3: _____

REMEMBER: Any physical space has many details. Training yourself to select only the most dominant details helps you to separate the important from the unimportant.

PATTERN 6: COMPARISON AND CONTRAST

Is the following paragraph a comparison or a contrast?

Example

My new school is quite different from my old. First, it's in a nicer neighborhood, while my old one was in a poor section of the city. Second, the teachers here seem so much more interested, compared to the turned-off teachers I remember so well. Third, there's more opportunity to have friends and a better social life, more so than in the junior high I used to attend. My new school certainly has many more advantages.

Analysis Is the writer showing similarities or differences? Note the details.

New school	**Old school**
In a nicer neighborhood	In a poor section of the city
Teachers seem more interested	Turned-off teachers
More opportunity to have friends and a better social life	Fewer friends and less social life

The three details given indicate the intent of the writing: to show differences between the two schools. Therefore, the paragraph may be called a contrast.

Learning to Organize Your Ideas

*A **contrast** between two places, two people, or two things aims to show how one is different from the other.*

*A **comparison**, on the other hand, conveys how two places, two people, or two things are similar.*

Now read this paragraph and determine whether it is a comparison or a contrast.

Example

The dog I bought recently resembles my first. She has the same white color as Shag, is as cute of manner, and loves to cuddle close. Just as Shag was friendly and licked everyone, Lucky is all over people when they enter the house. It's nice to have a dog that recaptures an old love.

Analysis   Examine the details given first.

Lucky	Shag
White color	White color
Cute	Cute
Cuddles close	Cuddles close
All over people	Friendly and licky

If you look at these details, it is obvious that both dogs are very close in appearance and manner. Therefore, we can conclude the writer wished to make a *comparison*.

REMEMBER: *Comparisons* show similarities, while *contrasts* show differences.

Test (See answers on page 246.)

Directions

Now think of a contrast you would like to make concerning two friends you have. List three details.

Friend 1	Friend 2
Detail 1: _____	Detail 1: _____
Detail 2: _____	Detail 2: _____
Detail 3: _____	Detail 3: _____

Write a paragraph that includes these contrasting qualities.

4

WRITING THE BUSINESS LETTER OF COMPLAINT

This section deals with how to write a business letter of complaint. There are, of course, many situations in life that require this type of letter. Your complaint may be in reaction to poor service, to false advertising, to inferior quality in a product you purchase, to rules you may think are unfair, to an action taken by a Congressman, or to a purchased item that got lost in the mail.

Whatever the reason for the complaint, the form of the letter you write is always the same. The Regents Competency Test in Writing requires, in addition to use of the acceptable letter form, a clear and effective written presentation.

In this section you will be shown, by example and application, how to combine both form and content—the what and the how—into a successful letter of complaint.

Writing the Business Letter of Complaint

Essentially, the form of any letter of complaint you write should be as follows:

MODEL
Letter of Complaint

	(Street address)	HEADING:
	(City, State, Zip code)	*Your address*
	(Date)	*and the date*

INSIDE ADDRESS: *The address of the company*
(Company, representative)
(Company name)
(Street address)
(City, State, Zip code)

SALUTATION: *The person to whom you are writing*
Dear . . . _____ :

PARAGRAPH 1: *Your purpose in writing*
_____
_____
_____
_____.

PARAGRAPH 2: *Supporting your purpose in writing*
_____
_____
_____
_____
_____.

PARAGRAPH 3: *Concluding your letter*
_____
_____
_____
_____
_____.

Very truly yours,	COMPLIMENTARY CLOSE
(Signature)	SIGNATURE
(Name)	NAME

NOTE: Most letters lend themselves to a *chronological approach*—what happened first, what happened second, etc. However, some problem situations may be better described by arranging the details in other patterns: *ascending order, descending order,* or *cause and effect.* The lessons in this chapter offer examples of all of the above.

BUSINESS LETTER CHECKLIST

Whatever the basis for your letter of complaint, be sure you include the following information:

Form

1. The writer's name and address and the date.
2. The reader's name, title, and address.
3. A complimentary close and signature.

Content

1. A statement of the problem.
2. Evidence, facts, information to support this statement.
3. A statement of how the problem should be resolved.
4. Reference to specific situations.
5. Reference to other people involved.

Specific Details

1. Name of the product purchased.
2. Model number, cost.
3. When and where product purchased.
4. Dates of calls, transactions, visits.
5. History of the problem.
6. Attempts to correct the problem.

Organization

1. An opening paragraph that defines and explains the reason for the complaint.
2. One or more paragraphs in which the background of the problem is clarified.
3. A final paragraph in which the correction is recommended.

Tone

1. A courteous, respectful, but firm approach.

THINKING THROUGH PROBLEM SITUATIONS

Study the following situations and decide what information you would supply in a letter of complaint. Outline an opening statement and support it with specific details. Then suggest a solution.

Situation 1: Each morning you notice beer cans and clumps of garbage all over your lawn. Since this has been a repeated problem, you wish to complain to your local police.

Situation 2: Your neighbor's dog barks all night and prevents you from sleeping. Even after talking to your neighbor, you find that the dog continues to disturb you. You decide to communicate by letter.

Situation 3: You work with someone who bosses you and takes unfair advantage at every opportunity. You have tried to talk with him, but he refuses to listen. Now you are ready to register your complaint with a supervisor.

Situation 4: You have ordered and received a new dishwasher. Already, there have been three servicemen at your house to repair the switches, but it still doesn't operate well. You wish to write to the service manager.

Situation 5: You are charged by a store for an item you never purchased. You call many times, but the bills, with added interest, keep coming. You plan to write to have this charge removed.

Outlines of Problem Situations

The following outlines provide a basis for responding to the problem situations given on this page.

Situation 1

    Opening Statement: It is a disgraceful situation to find my lawn littered almost daily.

    Details: Beer cans, clumps of garbage.

Situation 2

    Opening Statement: I would appreciate your exercising more control over your dog.

    Details: Neighbor's dog's barking, loss of sleep.

Situation 3

    Opening Statement: I feel I must convey to you an annoying situation concerning a fellow worker.

    Details: Being taken advantage of, being bossed, attempts to discuss the matter.

Situation 4

    Opening Statement: I am writing to complain that my new dishwasher, never properly serviced, is not operating well.

    Details: Three service calls, repeated failure.

Situation 5

    Opening Statement: It is distressing to be charged for an item I never purchased.

    Details: Bills received repeatedly, added interest.

Lesson 1

COMPLAINING ABOUT AN UNDESERVED TRAFFIC TICKET

THE WRITING TASK

On December 11, 1982, as you are driving past a traffic light, a policeman pulls you over and gives you a ticket for going through a red light. You explain that the light had already turned green as you were passing through, but he insists you were clearly wrong. You have a choice of either paying a $10 fine or appearing in court to argue your case before the judge.

Write a letter of complaint to the traffic court, registering your claim that you are not guilty of the traffic violation.

ANALYSIS OF THE TASK

What Are You Being Asked to Do?

To compose a letter of complaint about an unwarranted traffic ticket.

Writing the Business Letter of Complaint

How to Respond

Clarify the traffic situation in which you were judged wrongly, offering evidence that you are in the right.

THE MODEL

Heading
10-09 Williams Road
San Diego, CA 94107
December 29, 1982

Inside address
Municipal Traffic Court
60 Baxter Road
San Diego, CA 94107

Salutation
Dear Sirs:

The traffic ticket I received on December 11 is unjustified. The police officer claims I went through a red light, but I maintain the light had already changed when I drove through.

PARAGRAPH 1: *Clear statement of the reason for writing*

Transitionals*
First, another car had already gone through before me when the officer pulled me over. Second, when I explained that I was already through, the officer replied, *Direct quotations* "That may be, but it happens all the time." Third and most important, as the officer was writing, a passerby said, "Officer, I saw everything, and he didn't go through the light."

PARAGRAPH 2: *Evidence arranged in ascending order*

It isn't the $10 that bothers me; it's the principle of the matter. Why should I be fined for what I didn't do?

PARAGRAPH 3: *Concluding restatement of position*

Respectfully yours,

Jack Jones

Jack Jones

Complimentary close
Signature

---

*Note Throughout this book, marginal comments are keyed to the materials in the models. For example, in this letter, the marginal comment <u>transitionals</u> indicates that all transitionals in the model will be marked with a wavy line.

Writing the Business Letter of Complaint

Basic Components

This letter of complaint contains the following:

Structure:	Three distinct but connected paragraphs.
Content:	Three concrete pieces of evidence to support the complaint, in *ascending order* (the last one being the most important).
Conviction:	The tone of the letter suggests a strong basis for the writer's claim that he is in the right.
Organization:	The pattern of the letter is smooth, coherent, and logical.

Evaluation

This letter is a commendable response to a traffic-ticket situation because it

1. Follows an acceptable business form.
2. Presents necessary evidence.
3. Explains the situation clearly and directly.
4. Organizes the reasons for the complaint convincingly (*ascending order*).
5. Uses transitionals to connect paragraphs: "first," "second," "third."
6. Uses direct quotations, such as "Officer . . . he didn't go through the light," to strengthen the complaint.

FOLLOW-UP EXERCISES

Imagine you have been stopped by a policeman for speeding on a highway. The officer says you have been going 65 miles an hour, but you claim you have been going only 55 miles an hour. Write a letter of complaint to your local traffic court supporting your claim that you were not speeding. Be sure to include the following:

1. Separate paragraphs for each new idea.
2. Evidence in your favor.
3. Direct quotations to strengthen your complaint.

Final Analysis

Tickets are sometimes given to motorists wrongly. If this happens to you, you have a right to state your case in writing, provided that you can prove your contentions. The important consideration is that you present facts, not opinion.

Lesson 2

COMPLAINING ABOUT A TICKET MIX-UP

THE WRITING TASK

You have sent a check for $20 for two tickets for a November 7 performance of a famous rock group. The theater has sent you two tickets for November 14. You have called to change the tickets, but the theater has not sent you the tickets for the proper performance.

Write a letter of complaint in which you try to clarify the error and thus receive the proper tickets.

ANALYSIS OF THE TASK

What Are You Being Asked to Do?

Write a letter of complaint to a theater to correct an error regarding tickets for a rock performance.

How to Respond

Establish the error the theater has made, giving all the details of the inconveniences that resulted, so that you will receive the proper

Writing the Business Letter of Complaint

tickets in time to attend the performance. The structure of the letter should be:

Paragraph 1: A clear statement of the error.
Paragraph 2: Instances of inconvenience resulting from the error, the details arranged in *ascending order*.
Paragraph 3: An appeal for a quick response.

THE MODEL

                                 45 Henry Street
                                 Brooklyn, NY 11207   *Heading*
                                 September 5, 1983

Inside address   Nassau Coliseum
                    125 Hempstead Turnpike
                    Hempstead, NY 11530

Salutation   Dear Sirs:

Complex sentences

    There is an error in the tickets sent me for the Blazing Saddle rock concert. Though I clearly asked for two tickets for the November 7 performance, I received, instead, two for the one on November 14.

PARAGRAPH 1: *Statement of the ticket error*

    Your error has caused me much inconvenience. For one thing, having looked forward to seeing this fantastic group, I am worried I will not have the opportunity. Further, since I am so busy with my work schedule, November 7 is the only night I can attend. Most important, I need the tickets for November 7 because I promised my girlfriend that we would celebrate her birthday on that day, and I certainly don't want to disappoint her.

PARAGRAPH 2: *Three inconveniences arranged in ascending order*

Most important inconvenience

46

Writing the Business Letter of Complaint

    Therefore, I am returning the two November 14 tickets in exchange for two for November 7. Kindly send me the tickets as soon as possible.

                Very truly yours,

                Bill Blake

                Bill Blake

PARAGRAPH 3: An appeal to correct the error

Complimentary close

Signature

Basic Components

This letter contains the following:

Paragraph 1: An explanation of the error.
Paragraph 2: Three inconveniences that resulted, arranged in *ascending order*.
Paragraph 3: An appeal to correct the error as soon as possible.

Evaluation

This letter of complaint about a ticket mix-up is convincing because it

1. Follows an acceptable business form.
2. Explains the error clearly.
3. Shows how the error resulted in major inconveniences.
4. Arranges the inconveniences in a convincing manner, by *ascending order*.
5. Uses a number of complex sentences.
6. Contains sentence variety.
7. Employs parenthetical words, such as "instead" and "most important."

FOLLOW-UP EXERCISE

It is not unusual for theaters to make mistakes with regard to tickets for concerts. Since they are responsible for thousands of tickets for many performances, there is a possibility of error. That is why you should check carefully when you receive your tickets to see that they are for the right date. If not, it is imperative to exchange them immediately.

A business letter of complaint, written for the express purpose of correcting the error, can be effective. But if you write such a letter, be sure to pattern it as follows:

Paragraph 1: A direct explanation of the error.
Paragraph 2: Major inconveniences as a result of the error, arranged in *ascending order*.
Paragraph 3: An urgent request to have the error corrected.

Let us suppose you sent $40 for two tickets for a matinee performance of *Annie* for May 9. Instead, you receive two tickets for the May 9 evening performance. Write a letter of complaint in which you state the error, support it by stating the major inconveniences it caused, and conclude with an appeal for a quick resolution.

Final Analysis

Because of the large number of sales that theaters handle, ticket mix-ups are not unusual. Therefore, it is a simple matter of explaining the confusion over dates. Remember, be direct, factual, and business-like.

Lesson 3

COMPLAINING ABOUT A SCHOOL REGULATION

THE WRITING TASK

Your school has a regulation that students must eat their lunch inside the building. The principal has announced that there will be no exceptions and that if a student is found leaving the school during a lunch period, he or she will be punished.

Write a letter of complaint to your school principal in which you outline your reasons for feeling that the regulation should be abolished.

ANALYSIS OF THE TASK

What Are You Being Asked to Do?

Compose a letter of complaint about a school regulation that you consider unfair.

How to Respond

Establish at the beginning why you are writing to the principal and present convincing reasons why the regulation should be abolished. The structure of the letter should be:

Paragraph 1: Why you are writing.

Writing the Business Letter of Complaint

Paragraph 2: Three convincing reasons, arranged in *descending order* of importance.

Paragraph 3: An alternate solution to the current regulation.

THE MODEL

Heading
101 Steele Avenue
Queens, NY 10540
April 6, 1983

Inside address
Dr. Frank Wilbur, Principal
Jay Adams High School
11 Flushing Boulevard
Queens, NY 10540

Salutation
Dear Dr. Wilbur:

Our school regulation requiring students to eat lunch only in the cafeteria is unfair. Going outdoors to eat lunch has many advantages.

PARAGRAPH 1: School regulation is unfair

Transitionals
<u>Most important</u>, our school cafeteria is crowded, filthy, and unpleasant. So many students bunched together in one place creates an unwholesome atmosphere. <u>Also,</u> the food served has no variety. The daily menu has starchy foods that have little nutritional value. <u>In addition,</u> restricting students to one space is dangerous and unhealthy.

PARAGRAPH 2: Three supporting reasons given in descending order

<u>For these reasons</u>, I believe the present rule should be replaced by one that allows the students to eat in one area on the campus lawn.

PARAGRAPH 3: Alternate solution

Very truly yours,

Betty Blake

Betty Blake

Complimentary close

Signature

Writing the Business Letter of Complaint

Basic Components

This letter contains the following:

Paragraph 1:   A clear statement that the school regulation is unfair.
Paragraph 2:   Three significant reasons why a change is needed.
Paragraph 3:   A recommended change.

Evaluation

This letter of complaint about a school regulation is notable because it

1. Follows an acceptable business form.
2. Focuses directly on a problem.
3. Presents reasoned support for a needed change in school policy.
4. Organizes that reasoned support in *descending order* of importance.
5. Uses transitionals to bridge sentences ("also," "in addition") and paragraphs ("for these reasons").
6. Employs a variety of adjectives ("crowded," "filthy," "unpleasant").

FOLLOW-UP EXERCISE

Every school has many rules and regulations that cause student reaction. In the above instance it was a particular regulation that made one student react. Now think of another school regulation that displeases you. Compose a letter of complaint convincing your principal that this regulation should be changed. Be sure to structure your letter this way:

Paragraph 1:   A clear statement about the school regulation.
Paragraph 2:   Three supporting reasons arranged in *descending order* (the most important stated first).
Paragraph 3:   What you would see as a welcome change.

Final Analysis

Not all school rules are popular, of course. Most of them are implemented to provide safety and security for the majority of students. As a result, some may be displeasing to individual students.

You have a right, therefore, to express your honest convictions to your school principal, who most likely will welcome your input. Since rules are flexible and sometimes need to be changed, your principal may indeed listen carefully to what you have to offer.

Be honest, direct, and informative, never insulting or opinionated.

Lesson 4

COMPLAINING ABOUT LOST BAGGAGE

THE WRITING TASK

You have just returned on TWA Flight No. 511 from Los Angeles. Upon retrieving your baggage, you find one valise missing. An attendant from the TWA desk searches everywhere, but apparently your valise is lost.

Write a letter of complaint in which you report the loss of your valise and all the discomforts that have resulted.

ANALYSIS OF THE TASK

What Are You Being Asked to Do?

Write a letter of complaint in which you report the loss of your valise.

How to Respond

Provide all the particulars of your flight, a description of your bag, and a summary of the discomforts you had to face.

Writing the Business Letter of Complaint

THE MODEL

                                                  1115 East Brown Street   *Heading*
                                                  Union, NJ 90456
                                                  February 4, 1983

Inside address   Consumer Complaint Division
                       TWA Office
                       Kennedy Airport
                       Queens, NY 11305

Salutation   Gentlemen:

                        The loss of my valise on your Flight   PARAGRAPH 1:
                   No. 511 from Los Angeles to Kennedy on   *The loss and*
                   February 3 has caused me considerable   *the flight*
                   discomfort.

                        <u>Worst of all</u> is that the valise in   PARAGRAPH 2:
                   question contains 10 rolls of film, the   *Three*
                   loss of which is extremely distressing.   *discomforts,*
                   Without these pictures, I have no   *arranged in*
Transitionals   record of my trip. <u>Second,</u> the valise,   *descending*
                   a Craemer leather type, is brand new.   *order*
                   <u>Third,</u> it was a gift from my mother for
                   my birthday and is worth well over
                   $100.

                        <u>As you can see,</u> your negligence in   PARAGRAPH 3:
                   misplacing this valise has caused great   *The urgency*
                   distress. Since it means so much to me   *of locating,*
                   personally, replacing it with another   *not replacing,*
                   will not be satisfactory. Please notify   *the valise*
                   me as soon as you locate it.

                                        Respectfully yours,   *Complimentary*
                                          Fernando Lopez   *close*
                                          Fernando Lopez   *Signature*

Writing the Business Letter of Complaint

Basic Components

This letter of complaint is exemplary because it contains the following:

1. A report of the loss in Paragraph 1.
2. An outline of major inconveniences or discomforts suffered from the loss, arranged in *descending order*.
3. As a conclusion, an urgent appeal to locate, not replace, the valise.
4. A consistent tone of distress.

Evaluation

This letter is also exemplary because it contains the following:

1. An acceptable business form.
2. A clear statement of the problem upon which the letter is based.
3. An emphasis on the discomforts and sense of personal loss caused by the mistake.
4. Transitionals such as "worst of all," "second," "third," "as you can see." (These phrases provide a smooth flow from one idea to another.)
5. Paragraph divisions that are in logical order.
6. A statement of discomforts in *descending order*, with the most serious one stated first: "Worst of all is that the valise in question contains 10 rolls of film, the loss of which is extremely distressing."

FOLLOW-UP EXERCISE

Having returned from Paris on Pan Am Flight No. 502, arriving at Kennedy, you discover that your Meister brown suede camera bag is missing. Write a letter of complaint in which you carefully describe the bag, the distress caused by the loss, and what you expect the airline to do about it. Be sure to arrange your details in *descending order*. The structure may be:

Paragraph 1:   A clear description of the lost valise and identification of the flight taken.

Paragraph 2: The most serious discomfort, a second discomfort, and a third.
Paragraph 3: What you expect the airline to do.

Final Analysis

When baggage is lost, the first thing you should do is report it to the appropriate airline desk. An attendant will try to help you locate it. In some cases, it will be forwarded to you at a later date. But when it is really lost, a well-written letter of complaint just may bring results.

Be insistent, firm and personal.

Lesson 5

COMPLAINING ABOUT A LOST ORDER

THE WRITING TASK

On April 15 you sent some film in for developing. On May 1 you inquire why you haven't received your prints. The film processing company responds that your 20-exposure roll of Kodacolor II has been lost but that the company is making every effort to try to find it as soon as possible. One month later you still haven't received any word about your roll of film.

Write a letter of complaint to the film processing company, registering your concern about the roll of film that you sent in but never received. Address the letter to Western Processing, 89 North Road, Clayton, Delaware 54082.

ANALYSIS OF THE TASK

What Are You Being Asked to Do?

Compose a letter of complaint about a lost roll of film—a letter that will bring some positive action from the company.

Writing the Business Letter of Complaint

How to Respond

State clearly the reason why you are writing and support that reason with the details given above. Outline the letter as follows:

Paragraph 1: Purpose of the letter.
Paragraph 2: Background details of dates of mailing and letters sent.
Paragraph 3: An expression of how you feel and how you expect the company to respond.

THE MODEL

                           80 Exeter Road
                           Brooklyn, NY 11234   *Heading*
                           June 5, 1982

Inside address   Western Processing Company
                    89 North Road
                    Clayton, DE 54082

Salutation   Dear Sirs:

                I have waited long enough to write this letter. It has been almost two months since I first sent you a roll of film for developing, but I have heard nothing since.   **PARAGRAPH 1:** *Establishes a reason for the complaint*

Prepositional phrases   On April 15, I sent you one roll of Kodacolor II 20-exposure film. Three weeks later, on May 11, I inquired about the film and was told you would look for it. Now two months later, the developed pictures have still not arrived. Naturally, I am very concerned about these pictures, since they were taken at a special family party.   **PARAGRAPH 2:** *Strengthens that reason with details arranged chronologically*

Adverbial clause

Writing the Business Letter of Complaint

> I hope you will waste no time in locating the film and sending me the developed prints as soon as possible.
>
> Very truly yours,
>
> *Roger Ambrel*
>
> Roger Ambrel

PARAGRAPH 3: Emphasizes the need to find the film

Complimentary close

Signature

Basic Components

The above letter contains the following:

Paragraph 1: A clear statement of distress over the loss of film.
Paragraph 2: All the important information needed to explain what happened.
Paragraph 3: The writer's request that the company find the film.

Evaluation

This letter is a commendable response to the problem of the lost film because it

1. Follows an acceptable business form.
2. Gives information clearly and directly.
3. Presents a full picture of the problem.
4. Organizes the details of the problem as they arose (*chronologically*), to show continuity.
5. Uses prepositional phrases, such as "on April 15" and "on May 11," to stress the facts of the delay.
6. Uses adverbial clauses to indicate reasons for action.
7. Uses a variety of sentence structures, such as the compound:

> "It has been almost two months since I first sent you a roll of film for developing, but I have heard nothing since."

Two complete thoughts, joined by the conjunction "but," that emphasize the passage of time.

59

Writing the Business Letter of Complaint

FOLLOW-UP EXERCISE

Suppose you returned an electric toothbrush to the manufacturer for repair and had not received it back after a month. Having written to them, you are then told that the package was lost. Write a letter of complaint in which you tell not only how you feel but also include a full accounting of dates and letters of inquiry. Be sure to pattern your letter after the following:

Paragraph 1: A clear statement of why you are writing.
Paragraph 2: All the details presented *chronologically*.
Paragraph 3: A statement of what you expect the company to do to rectify the problem.

Final Analysis

Companies that lose your personal items are not necessarily liable. They can claim it was the fault of the post office. Therefore, in framing your letter, avoid the "demand" approach in favor of the "urgent" tone. Be honest and forthright but avoid vulgarities. For example, "You'd better find the lousy toothbrush" should be changed to "I feel it's your responsibility to retrieve the lost toothbrush." Show, too, how important the item is to you.

Lesson 6

COMPLAINING ABOUT A MISLEADING AD

THE WRITING TASK

You purchase a product based on the following advertisement and find that it does not live up to the company's claims. Write a letter of complaint to the company, conveying your annoyance and displeasure.

> Send for your black-and-white runner's T-shirt made of durable cotton and designed to last. Washable and guaranteed nonshrinkable. Send $6.50 plus $1.00 for postage and handling to:
>
> JERRY ALLEN AND COMPANY
> 695 RENKIN AVENUE
> ALLENTOWN, PA 36201

Writing the Business Letter of Complaint

ANALYSIS OF THE TASK

What Are You Being Asked to Do?

To compose a letter of complaint about a runner's T-shirt you bought for $7.50 and found to be inferior to the product advertised.

How to Respond

List the reasons why the T-shirt was unsatisfactory. Outline them first as follows:

Reasons for the Complaint
1. The shirt tore on the first wearing.
2. The shirt shrank when washed.
3. The color began to run.

THE MODEL

	17 Ovington Road Dayton, OH 87035 May 7, 1982	*Heading*
Inside address	Jerry Allen and Company 695 Renkin Avenue Allentown, PA 36201	
Salutation	Dear Mr. Allen:	
	I am writing to request a refund on a black-and-white T-shirt which I purchased for $6.50 plus $1.00 for postage and handling. After wearing it for only one week, I find it completely unsatisfactory as to quality and am annoyed that it does not live up to the claims of the advertisement.	PARAGRAPH 1: *States the purpose of the letter—the nature of the complaint*
Transitionals	<u>First,</u> the T-shirt, on the first wearing, tore easily. <u>Second,</u> after it was washed, I found that it had shrunk and no longer fit me. <u>Last,</u> the original black color has faded because the dye ran.	PARAGRAPH 2: *Supports purpose with specific details, arranged chronologically*

Writing the Business Letter of Complaint

      Naturally, I am very distressed over this. Since the T-shirt fails to live up to your claims, I am returning it for a refund. Please send a refund check as soon as possible.

                      Respectfully yours,

                        Jerry Ames

                        Jerry Ames

PARAGRAPH 3: *Concludes with strong feeling and note of expectation*

Complimentary close

Signature

Basic Components

This letter contains the following:

Paragraph 1: A clear request for a refund on an item purchased.
Paragraph 2: Three convincing details arranged *chronologically*.
Paragraph 3: A concluding statement that establishes the writer's distress and desire for a refund.

Evaluation

This letter of complaint is superior because it

1. Follows an acceptable business form.
2. Is organized and coherent.
3. States its purpose in Paragraph 1.
4. Supports that purpose with reasons in Paragraph 2.
5. Concludes with a clear expectation.
6. Uses transitionals like "first," "second," "last."

FOLLOW-UP EXERCISE

On your own, write a similar letter of complaint about a sports game you purchased for $13.50 from Dutton and Sons, 118 East Avenue, Saddle River, NJ 07458. Cite three convincing reasons why the game has not lived up to the claims of the ad.

The plan of the letter should be as follows:

Paragraph 1: The purpose of writing the letter.
Paragraph 2: Three solid reasons to support your claim.
Paragraph 3: Your views as to how the company should respond to your complaint.

Final Analysis

When you complain about a product to a company, be sure you have good reason to do so, such as inferior quality, cheap workmanship, poor performance. Avoid generalities; cite specific examples and give the details of your dissatisfaction.

Lesson 7

COMPLAINING ABOUT AN INFERIOR PRODUCT

THE WRITING TASK

On March 8, you purchased a GE X-100 portable radio from a store for $87.59. You immediately discover that the radio's station dial is stuck. When you return to the store with the radio, the salesman sends you to the service division to have it repaired. On March 15, you pick up the radio and return home. You discover then that the radio is still defective in the same way.

Write a letter of complaint to the store where you bought the radio. In the letter, state clearly what the problem is and give specific information. Address the letter to: Eastern Electronics, 89-56 Mount Sinai Road, Bronx, New York 11546.

ANALYSIS OF THE TASK

What Are You Being Asked to Do?

Compose a letter of complaint about an item that was bought from a store, which turned out to be defective.

Writing the Business Letter of Complaint

How to Respond

State clearly the reason why you are writing the letter and support it with the facts provided. Outline the letter first, as follows:

1. Reason for writing.
2. Details to support that reason, that is, proof that the item is indeed defective.
3. Your expectation of how the store should respond.

THE MODEL

	198 Boynton Avenue Bronx, NY 11546 March 22, 1983	*Heading*
Inside address	Eastern Electronics 89-56 Mount Sinai Road Bronx, NY 11546	
Salutation	Dear Manager:	
Adverbial clauses	I am writing to express my annoyance over a radio that I bought in your store and returned for repair but which remains defective.	PARAGRAPH 1: *Gives a clear statement of the problem*
Prepositional phrases	On March 8, I purchased a GE X-100 portable for $87.59. When I returned home, I found that the station dial was stuck and would not move past a certain point. When I returned to the store, I was told to take the radio to your service division, where it would be repaired. One week later, on March 15, the radio was returned and, again, the station dial did not function.	PARAGRAPH 2: *Supports and strengthens the case with details on poor service (chronological listing)*

Writing the Business Letter of Complaint

I spent $87.59 for this radio and yet it doesn't work. I have also spent a lot of time going to and from your store. At this point, I expect you to take the radio back and replace it with a new one.

PARAGRAPH 3: Concludes on a note of annoyance and expectation

Respectfully yours,

Complimentary close

Jane Alexander

Signature

Jane Alexander

Basic Components

This letter contains the following:

Paragraph 1: A clear statement of the problem concerning a defective item purchased from a store.
Paragraph 2: An anecdotal record of the follow-up service.
Paragraph 3: An expression of the writer's annoyance.
Paragraph 4: A statement of what she wants the store to do for her.

Evaluation

The above letter is a successful response to a situation involving a defective item purchased in a store. It

1. Follows an acceptable business form.
2. Is clear and direct.
3. Organizes the details of poor service as they happened (*chronologically*), creating a consistent pattern that shows the full picture.
4. Uses adverbial clauses to show time sequences ("when I returned home," "when I returned to the store").
5. Uses prepositional phrases to show further time sequences ("on March 8," "one week later," "on March 15," "at this point").

FOLLOW-UP EXERCISE

On your own, write a similar letter of complaint to a store about a defective item that you purchased. Think of all the measures you have taken to get the problem rectified. List these measures in order of occurrence (*chronologically*). Use adverbial clauses and adverbial phrases to show time patterns.

The plan of the letter would be as follows:

Paragraph 1: A clear statement expressing annoyance over a defective item.
Paragraph 2: Evidence, in time order, of measures you have taken to get the item repaired or replaced.
Paragraph 3: What you expect the store to do now about the still defective item.

Final Analysis

When you write a letter of complaint to a store about a defective item, don't just tell them how annoyed or angry you are. Rather, give evidence—all the dates and steps you have taken—that shows clearly that the store has failed to stand behind its merchandise. In fact, if you convince the manager of the store that you have acted in good faith, the manager will probably respond quickly.

Lesson 8

COMPLAINING ABOUT AN INCIDENT IN A RESTAURANT

THE WRITING TASK

You go to a restaurant with your friends and find that the service is poor. The waitress takes a long time to bring your order, ignores you when you request water and bread, and does not follow up on your complaint that the main dish is cold.

In writing a letter of complaint to the restaurant, register your annoyance over the poor service. Address the letter to: West Diner, 10 Merrick Road, Patchogue, New York 11765.

ANALYSIS OF THE TASK

What Are You Being Asked to Do?

Compose a letter of complaint about a restaurant situation in which you were treated discourteously.

Writing the Business Letter of Complaint

How to Respond

State clearly the reason why you are writing and support it with actual evidence of discourtesy on the part of the waitress. Outline the letter first, as follows:

1. Reason for writing.
2. Details to support that reason.
3. Your views as to how the restaurant should resolve the problem.

THE MODEL

Heading

60 Greene Street
Patchogue, NY 11765
August 5, 1982

Inside address

Manager
West Diner
100 Merrick Road
Patchogue, NY 11765

Salutation

Dear Manager:

Transitional words

On the evening of August 3, my friends and I dined at your restaurant. Unfortunately, we were greatly disappointed with the service we received. We were particularly annoyed by the waitress who was called Joan by her fellow workers. She neglected our needs throughout the meal.

PARAGRAPH 1: *States the purpose of the letter*

When we <u>first</u> arrived, we were kept waiting before we could order. <u>Then</u>, when we had ordered, the waitress took a long time in bringing our food to the table. <u>Later</u>, when we requested water and bread, she ignored us. <u>Finally</u>, when I complained that the hamburger she had placed on the table was cold, she disappeared and did nothing about it.

PARAGRAPH 2: *Supports that purpose with concrete examples (chronological arrangement)*

Writing the Business Letter of Complaint

> This was an extremely unsatisfactory dining experience, and we feel that we are entitled to a complimentary dinner worth $5 to compensate us for our disappointment.
>
> Sincerely yours,
>
> *Alice Jones*
>
> Alice Jones

PARAGRAPH 3: Concludes with strong feeling and decisiveness

Complimentary close

Signature

Basic Components

This letter contains the following:

Paragraph 1: A clear statement of the problem being addressed.
Paragraph 2: Three specific examples of discourteous service.
Paragraph 3: A summary statement of the writer's displeasure.

Evaluation

This letter is an excellent response to a situation involving discourteous service because it

1. Follows an acceptable business form.
2. Is clear and direct.
3. Explains the situation convincingly.
4. Arranges the specific examples logically. In this case, the writer has chosen to be *chronological*; that is, she has cited the examples in the order in which they happened.
5. Uses transitional words such as: "first," "then," "later," "finally." These transitional (connecting) words help to place the examples in sequence.

FOLLOW-UP EXERCISE

On your own, write a similar letter of complaint about a situation in which you received discourteous service. Think of three examples to support your complaint and arrange them *chronologically*. Use transitional words to sequence them in order of occurrence.

The plan of the letter would be as follows:

Paragraph 1: A clear statement outlining the incident of discourtesy.
Paragraph 2: Three specific examples to support your complaint.
Paragraph 3: Your expectation of how the restaurant should respond.

Final Analysis

When you complain about poor or inefficient service in a restaurant—or in any other place—be sure you have evidence to support your claim. Avoid expressions of strong anger; instead, stick to the facts and explain them as you recall them. The more facts you present, the more convincing your letter of complaint will be and, as a result, the better your chances of receiving a response.

Lesson 9

COMPLAINING ABOUT AN INFLATED BILL

THE WRITING TASK

You receive a telephone bill that charges you for calls you never made. You call the telephone company to correct the error, but you continue to receive the same inflated bill.

Write a letter of complaint to the telephone company. Explain the error as clearly as you can and ask to have your bill adjusted.

ANALYSIS OF THE TASK

What Are You Being Asked to Do?

Write a letter of complaint to the telephone company about incorrect charges.

How to Respond

Present evidence as proof that you never made the calls for which you are being charged.

Writing the Business Letter of Complaint

THE MODEL

	45 Sandwich Lane *Heading*
Akron, OH 62059
January 5, 1983

Inside address   Ohio Telephone Company
90-87 Baldwin Avenue
Akron, OH 62059

Salutation   Gentlemen:

My current monthly telephone bill, $35.67, is incorrect and in need of adjustment.   *PARAGRAPH 1: States the purpose of the letter*

Transitional clause   When I received this bill on October 6, 1982, I immediately called your office and was told someone would look into it, but no one called me back. Again, on October 9, 1982, I called and spoke to Mr. Jones, who agreed that an error had been made. On October 15, the same bill of $35.67 was sent to my home. Since that time I have written a number of letters, but the same inflated bill continues to be sent.   *PARAGRAPH 2: Supports this purpose with details (chronologically)*

Transitional adverb

Transitional phrases

I have not paid this bill because it is absolutely incorrect. According to my records, the amount should be $24.98. Please make this adjustment and send me a bill reflecting this change.   *PARAGRAPH 3: Requests a needed correction*

Very truly yours,   *Complimentary close*

David Segal   *Signature*

David Segal

Basic Components

This letter of complaint contains the following:

1. A statement of purpose in Paragraph 1.
2. Supporting details in Paragraph 2.
3. A request for correction in Paragraph 3.
4. A *chronological* arrangement of calls made and letters sent.
5. A brief, direct, but courteous tone.

Evaluation

The above letter is successful because it

1. Follows an acceptable business form.
2. Clearly establishes the reason for the letter.
3. Supports that reason by telling of efforts made to correct the problem.
4. Uses transitions, such as "when I received this bill on October 6, 1982" (clause), "again" (adverb), "on October 15" (phrase), to bring ideas closer together.
5. Conveys the problem and the need for its correction convincingly.

FOLLOW-UP EXERCISE

You receive an electric bill for $87.82, though you have been away from the house for the month for which you are being billed. You wish to have this bill adjusted. Write a letter of complaint to your local lighting company. Your letter should (1) outline the problem, (2) give background information to support your complaint, and (3) ask for adjustment.

Final Analysis

Utility companies do not intentionally overcharge their customers. Because of the vast number of people they service and also because of the complexity of computers, errors are occasionally made. These errors are sometimes difficult to resolve because there may not be any one person with whom you can discuss them. Therefore, a letter of complaint, clearly and directly phrased, becomes a very useful instrument of communication. Always offer facts to support your complaint, along with the dates of your previous attempts to resolve the problem.

Lesson 10

COMPLAINING ABOUT AN UNRECEIVED PAYMENT

THE WRITING TASK

A major gasoline company, for which you have a credit card, claims you have not paid a bill of $98.98. When you check your records, you find that you have, in fact, paid the bill. You attempt to reach the company to correct the error, but the bills continue to arrive.

Write a letter of complaint to the company in which you attempt to prove that the bill has already been paid. Address the letter to: Shell Oil Company, 477 Richmond Road, Arlington, West Virginia 15030.

ANALYSIS OF THE TASK

What Are You Being Asked to Do?

Write a letter of complaint to a major oil company, showing that a bill for gasoline has already been paid.

Writing the Business Letter of Complaint

How to Respond

Support your claim with direct references to evidence that the bill being sent is an error on the company's part. The outline of the letter should be:

Paragraph 1: A description of the problem: the bill and the continued arrival of duplicate bills at your home.

Paragraph 2: Evidence of the steps you have taken to correct the error, such as proof of payment.

Paragraph 3: An appeal for the company to adjust your records and stop sending the bills.

THE MODEL

Heading

```
                              500 Ashton Place
                              Arlington, WV 10530
                              May 5, 1983
```

Inside address

```
Shell Oil Company
477 Richmond Road
Arlington, WV 15030
```

Salutation Dear Sirs:

Compound sentence

You have continued to bill me for $98.98, even though you have already received and cashed my check in that amount. *Simple sentence*: Obviously, your billing department is making an error.

PARAGRAPH 1: *Outlines company's error with regard to a paid bill*

Complex sentence

When the original bill came on March 4, I made out a check in the amount of $98.98 and sent it in right away. When the same bill arrived on March 18, I marked the invoice "Paid." Two weeks later, on March 25, the same bill came again, at which time I called your local office and was told the bill would be adjusted. But it never was, for the statements indicating that I owe $98.98 continue to arrive.

PARAGRAPH 2: *Gives chronological record of attempts to correct problem*

Writing the Business Letter of Complaint

> I hope this letter will finally bring a solution to this problem. Enclosed you will find a duplicate of the canceled check, dated March 5, which is sufficient proof that the bill was indeed paid.
>
>   Very truly yours,
>
>   *Daniel Stone*
>
>   Daniel Stone

PARAGRAPH 3: *Furnishes proof that bill was paid*

Complimentary close

Signature

Basic Components

This letter contains the following:

Paragraph 1: A clear indication that the company has made an error.
Paragraph 2: A history of attempts to correct the problem, arranged *chronologically*.
Paragraph 3: An indication of submitted proof, as well as a statement of how troublesome the matter has been.

Evaluation

This letter does a good job of trying to correct a billing problem because it

1. Follows an acceptable business form.
2. Presents a history of the problem.
3. Sets out in *chronological sequence* the details of previous attempts to correct the problem.
4. Uses three separate paragraphs to show full and complete ideas.
5. Uses a variety of sentence structures to make the letter more interesting, such as a
   simple sentence: "Obviously, your billing department is making an error."

Writing the Business Letter of Complaint

compound sentence:	"You have continued to bill me . . ." even though you have already received and cashed my check in that amount."
complex sentence:	"When the original bill came on March 4, I made out a check in the amount of $98.98 and sent it in right away."

6. Clearly proves an instance of error on the company's part.

FOLLOW-UP EXERCISE

Now write a similar letter of complaint about an error with regard to a bill. You purchase a stereo system from Gordon Electronics, 477 Hempstead Turnpike, Levittown, New York 11756. You pay for the item by check. Later, for a period of three months, the store keeps billing you for the amount you have already paid: $354.09. Write a letter of complaint in which you provide the background information to prove that the store is in error.

The structure of the letter should be:

Paragraph 1:	The problem: continued arrival of the bill at your home.
Paragraph 2:	Proof of the steps you have taken as well as evidence of payment.
Paragraph 3:	A request that the store stop sending bills to your home and that your records be cleared.

Final Analysis

When you purchase anything, it is always wise to keep the receipt as well as the sales slip. Since companies and stores do make errors, it is much easier to prove your case by enclosing a copy of the receipt or the sales slip. Often, a copy of the check itself will serve.

In writing this kind of letter, be sure to refer to any of the above, as they are clear proof.

Lesson 11

COMPLAINING ABOUT A TEACHER'S ATTITUDE

THE WRITING TASK

You have a math teacher who doesn't seem to like you. Though you get passing grades on quizzes and know your work well, the teacher finds reason to criticize you: your work habits, your preparation, your participation.

Write a letter of complaint to your math teacher in which you confront his attitude and how it affects you. Offer specific evidence of the effects.

ANALYSIS OF THE TASK

What Are You Being Asked to Do?

To phrase a letter of complaint about the attitude of a math teacher.

How to Respond

Confront the attitude by showing how it affects you as a student.

Writing the Business Letter of Complaint

THE MODEL

Inside address

Salutation

Incident reference words

89 Kissena Boulevard
Flushing, NY 11435
January 30, 1983

Heading

Mr. Jerome Crater
Jay Adams High School
98-09 Jay Street
Flushing, NY 11435

Dear Mr. Crater:

    It seems clear to me your attitude about my work is negative, and I have been affected by this in a number of ways.

PARAGRAPH 1: *Confronts the teacher's attitude as a cause*

    While formerly I enjoyed math, I am losing interest in the subject now. For instance, that time I showed you a geometric solution, you told me I wasn't thinking clearly and that I should stop being so lazy. Another instance is the time I passed in a homework assignment that you criticized in front of the class. A third example of your negative attitude occurred when I answered a question in class and was told to think before I speak. All this was embarrassing to me.

PARAGRAPH 2: *Shows the effects of this attitude*

    Math is a subject I can learn. But if you constantly criticize me, as you have, I will not be able to do well in your class. For these reasons, I would like to speak with you at your convenience.

PARAGRAPH 3: *Appeals to the teacher to discuss the matter*

Very truly yours,

Jane Seymour

Jane Seymour

Complimentary close

Signature

Basic Components

This letter of complaint contains the following:

Structure: Three distinct, related paragraphs.
Content: Three instances, in Paragraph 2, showing a *cause-effect relationship*, arranged to show how the teacher's attitude (cause) lowers the student's self-esteem (effect).
Conviction: The tone of the letter suggests a deeply felt hurt on the part of the student and a conviction that the problem can be dealt with.
Organization: The flow of the letter is smooth: from a statement of the problem, to a presentation of specific instances, to a desire to resolve the matter.

Evaluation

This letter is exemplary because it

1. Follows an acceptable business form.
2. Clearly states the basis for the complaint.
3. Supports that basis with three concrete instances of the teacher's attitude (arranged in a *cause-effect pattern*).
4. Uses incident reference words: "for instance," "another instance," "a third example." These words help to draw attention to events that have already happened.
5. Deals with the problem in a positive manner, requesting an opportunity to resolve it.

FOLLOW-UP EXERCISE

Select one teacher you feel had an attitude toward you that affected your work in a particular subject. Write a letter of complaint in which you show how the attitude is directly related to your performance in class. Be sure to include the following:

1. Three separate but related paragraphs.
2. Incident reference words to draw attention to specific situations.

3. A positive approach to the problem and a request to meet to deal with it.
4. A clear indication of *cause and effect*.

Final Analysis

While they are trained to be helpful and considerate, some teachers occasionally act in ways which might be interpreted as insensitive. In such cases it is reasonable to register an honest reaction (*result*) to that behavior (*cause*). This approach may result in a new beginning for you.

Be honest and direct, but never insulting. Show that you are mature in your own attitude.

Lesson 12

COMPLAINING ABOUT AN UNSATISFACTORY TRAVEL EXPERIENCE

THE WRITING TASK

You sign up with a charter group for a trip to Colombia, South America. The group promises, in addition to the flight and accommodations, a special visit to a famous historic site. When you get there, however, you are told that there will be no such visit.

Write a letter of complaint to Essex Travel, 110 Fourth Avenue, New York 11320 in which you convey how unsatisfactory you found the trip because the group did not live up to its promise.

ANALYSIS OF THE TASK

What Are You Being Asked to Do?

Write a letter of complaint to a travel group that has failed to live up to its agreement.

Writing the Business Letter of Complaint

How to Respond

Establish exactly what it is that the group has omitted and show how this omission affected the quality of your experience. Plan the letter as follows:

Paragraph 1: A clear explanation of what the group has omitted and how disappointed you are.
Paragraph 2: The effects and how they spoiled the experience.
Paragraph 3: What you expect of the group at this time.

THE MODEL

Heading

14 Star Drive
Jamaica, NY 11435
March 5, 1983

Inside address

Essex Travel
110 Fourth Avenue
New York City, NY 11320

Salutation

Dear Sirs:

Your February 18-25 charter trip to Colombia, South America, was a terrible disappointment to me. While the contract I signed promised an excursion to the ruins of Fudor, our group was never taken there. Although we were not taken to Fudor, we received no compensation.

PARAGRAPH 1: *The basis for writing—disappointment in a trip (the cause)*

Transitionals to show effects

As a result, my deep interest in ancient ruins was never satisfied. One of the reasons for my going on this trip was the promise of seeing historic Fudor. In addition, our failure to visit the site caused a great deal of confusion in the group, as we constantly challenged our tour leader

PARAGRAPH 2: *The effects of this disappointment*

Writing the Business Letter of Complaint

Transitionals to show effects — to be more explicit about the details of the trip. <u>Furthermore</u>, when we questioned the tour leader about compensation for not going to Fudor, he remained silent and totally uncooperative.

<u>Unfortunately</u>, for the above reasons, our trip to Colombia was a frustrating one. Since you did not live up to the letter of the contract, I am requesting that $50 of the total price of the trip be returned as compensation.

PARAGRAPH 3: A request for a return of money

Very truly yours,

Murray Barkin

Murray Barkin

Complimentary close

Signature

Basic Components

This letter has the following essentials:

Paragraph 1: An expression of disappointment because of the uncompleted itinerary.
Paragraph 2: Three significant effects on the writer and the others in the group.
Paragraph 3: A request for compensation based on the terms of the contract.

Evaluation

This letter of complaint about an unsatisfactory travel experience is convincing because it

1. Follows an acceptable business form.
2. Focuses consistently on an omission.

3. Shows how this omission affected the writer and the others in the group.
4. Arranges the details in a *cause-effect pattern*.
5. Uses a variety of sentence structures.
6. Employs key transitional words—such as "as a result," "in addition," "furthermore," and "unfortunately"—to highlight the effect.
7. Provides a solution at the end.

FOLLOW-UP EXERCISE

You sign up for a charter trip on Delta Airlines, to Miami Beach, Florida. You are told in the contract that three meals will be provided. Instead, you find that only two meals are actually served.

Write a letter of complaint to Delta Airlines, 110 Fifth Avenue, New York, NY 11209, in which you complain about the omission and how it affected you and others. At the end, provide a solution to the problem.

Final Analysis

It is not uncommon for travelers to find that charter trips fall short of the promises made by their organizers. Since it is impossible to deal with the problem while you are in a foreign country, it is more expedient to wait until you return to complain about it. Writing to the airline or the travel group can be an effective follow-up. But be sure to show exactly what was omitted and how that omission created not only frustration but, generally, an unsatisfactory experience.

5
WRITING THE REPORT

Most people can give a report orally but find that writing one is another matter. A written report requires accurate details, properly arranged and expressed.

A report is a record of an event that has already happened. As the writer, it is your job to study the notes you have taken and to decide how they should be organized. Depending on the event, they can be organized (1) chronologically, (2) by contrast and comparison, (3) spatially, (4) by cause and effect, (5) in declining order of importance, or (6) in ascending order of importance.

The purpose of this section is to show you, by application and example, how best to arrange and organize recorded notes so that your written report will be clear, accurate, and convincing. This will help you to improve your reporting skills and will also make you a better writer in general.

Writing the Report

REPORT CHECKLIST

Whatever the subject of your report, be sure that you cover the following.

Arrangements

Determine the best order of details based on the situation. For example:

1. **Chronological Order:** Arranging events in order of the time at which they occurred—what happened first, what happened second, what happened third, etc.
2. **Contrast and Comparison:** Showing how one situation is like another (comparison) or showing how one situation is different from another (contrast).
3. **Spatial Order:** Describing the details around you in a particular place. What are the most conspicuous details I see here?
4. **Cause and Effect:** Showing that there is a relationship between a situation and the people involved. How does the situation affect the people?
5. **Ascending Order:** Arranging details in an order of importance so that the most significant one comes last. What is one important detail, a second, a third, and, finally, the most important?
6. **Descending Order:** Arranging details in an order of importance so that the most significant one comes first. What is the most important detail, a second, a third, etc.?

THINKING THROUGH REPORT SITUATIONS

Now study the following situations and decide which arrangement you would use in reporting on each one. Decide which arrangement of details you will use, then organize these details accordingly.

Situation 1: You are asked to question your neighbors regarding their views about increased taxes. You will hear both sides of the issue.

Situation 2: You are asked to attend a concert in your school auditorium. You will report on the performance and the reaction of the audience.

89

Writing the Report

Situation 3: You are asked to report on a trip you took to a famous historic site. You are to describe the highlights of what you saw.

Situation 4: You are asked to visit the location of a tragic fire that caused a great deal of destruction. You are to report the reactions of the residents.

Situation 5: You are asked to canvass your schoolmates on a new suspension regulation. Your goal is to list the reasons why many are opposed.

Answers
Situation 1: Contrast.
Situation 2: Cause and effect.
Situation 3: Spatial order.
Situation 4: Cause and effect.
Situation 5: Ascending or descending order.

Lesson 1

REPORTING ON A TALK BY AN EX-STUDENT

THE WRITING TASK

A former student at your school who has become famous as an actor is invited to speak in the auditorium. The purpose of the meeting is to show how hard work, purpose, and dedication can lead to fame and success. Your teacher has asked that while you are listening to the speaker, you take notes for a class report. The notes you took are in the box on the next page.

Writing the Report

> **NOTES ON A TALK BY AN EX-STUDENT**
>
> Bob Larat spoke about his former schooldays
> The speaker was to appear early in the auditorium
> Bob Larat explained what it's like to be an actor
> All the senior classes were invited to hear him
> He looked quite handsome, very important
> He cried when he referred to his family life
> The talk lasted one full period
> The audience sat enthralled by what he said
> Bob Larat was introduced by the principal
> Students asked many questions about his life
> When the talk was over, no one wanted to leave
> He emphasized the importance of making plans for the future
> Bob Larat is seen weekly on a TV series

Arrange all these notes into a final written form. In your report, be certain to:

1. Group and develop all notes into a specific pattern.
2. Write complete sentences.
3. Edit your writing for correctness.

ANALYSIS OF THE TASK

What Are You Being Asked to Do?

Write a fully developed report on a talk by an ex-student, using the notes given.

How to Respond

Read all the notes carefully to see how they should be grouped. Then, when you see a plan, rearrange them accordingly. In this case, aim for an *ascending order*, in which the most important part of the talk is reserved for last. Where possible, expand more fully on any of the notes.

Writing the Report

THE MODEL

Report on a Talk by an Ex-Student

On March 4, 1983, all the senior classes were invited to the auditorium to hear Bob Larat, a former student who became a famous actor, speak about his student days and how they paved the way to an acting career. Having arrived early, he was led to the stage by the principal, introduced, and presented as an inspiration to all.

PARAGRAPH 1: Background and preparation of event

As he stood before us, he looked quite handsome, and very important. He began his talk with a look back to his student days, when he used to get into trouble for cutting classes. The audience seemed surprised by this. Then he expanded on what it's like to be an actor today. Later, he emphasized the importance of making plans for the future. Finally, the most dramatic moment came when he referred to his family life: how he grew up on the streets, how his parents neglected him, how he was pretty much on his own as a young child. As he described this period in his life, he cried.

Transitionals

PARAGRAPH 2: Highlights of talk by speaker, details arranged in ascending order

When the talk was over, no one wanted to leave. Students were eager to ask many questions, especially about his role on a well-known TV series. This was a most stimulating talk by a very important person.

PARAGRAPH 3: The effect of the talk on the audience

Basic Components

This report on a talk by an ex-student rates high because it provides the following:

Paragraph 1: Background of and preparation for the event.
Paragraph 2: Coverage of the highlights of the talk by Bob Larat.
Paragraph 3: The effect of the talk on the audience.

Evaluation

This report is well done because it

1. Uses all the notes given.
2. Arranges the notes according to an *ascending order* pattern, the last item being the most important.
3. Fleshes out certain notes to provide fuller descriptions.
4. Uses a variety of sentence types.
5. Uses transitionals such as "as he stood before us," "then," and "later."
6. Is structurally sound and free of mechanical errors.

FOLLOW-UP EXERCISE

Recording the talks of special speakers is a common task. Although it is tempting to take down everything the speaker says, it is more important—so as not to bore the reader—to monitor the highlights of the talk. Saving the most dramatic moment for last (*ascending order*) adds zest to your writing.

Select a student in your school who is well known or popular. Arrange to have an interview with that student in which you ask prepared questions. Take notes as you listen and arrange these notes in *ascending order*.

Final Analysis

Good reporting depends on good note-taking—a skill that requires repeated use. Only after a series of notes have been written down can a decision be made on what is most important. Therefore, study all your notes and choose to write about those that you consider to be of greatest interest to your audience.

Lesson 2

REPORTING ON AN INTERVIEW WITH THE SCHOOL PRINCIPAL

THE WRITING TASK

Along with other students, you have been asked to appear in the principal's office to interview him on a new dress code. You are to use your notes to complete a report to be read before other students in your grade. The notes you have recorded are in the box on the next page.

Writing the Report

> **NOTES ON AN INTERVIEW WITH THE SCHOOL PRINCIPAL**
>
> We chatted about the dress code before he entered
> The interview lasted a half-hour
> We met in his office on the main floor
> It was a very pleasant meeting, very open
> I read my report one week later to other students
> He finally emphasized that proper attire creates a better climate for learning
> At first he discussed the need for the code
> Mr. Atkins is a tall, impressive man
> Second, he expressed his concern about the students' informality
> He also referred to standards needed in a young person's life
> All the interviewers posed many questions
> He praised us for our interest and involvement

Arrange all these notes into a final written form. In your report, be certain to:

1. Group and develop all notes.
2. Write complete sentences.
3. Edit your writing for correctness.

ANALYSIS OF THE TASK

What Are You Being Asked to Do?

Write a fully developed report on an interview with a school principal, using the notes given. The completed report is to be given to other students in your grade.

How to Respond

Study the notes carefully to see what the best pattern would be. In this case, group the notes in an *ascending order*—first important observation, next important observation, and finally the most important observation of the principal's talk. This pattern will create a more effective report because it saves the most important reason for last. Where possible, expand further on any of the notes.

THE MODEL

Report on an Interview with the Principal

Combining notes

I was one of several students assigned to report to the principal's office on the main floor to interview Mr. Atkins, a tall, impressive man who conducted a very pleasant, open meeting. Since our purpose was to chat about the dress code he wishes to implement in the school, all the interviewers posed many questions.

PARAGRAPH 1: *The scene of the interview, its purpose, a description of the principal*

Expanding on notes

At first, he discussed the need for a dress code, pointing out how few rules and regulations are respected nowadays. Second, he expressed his concern about the informality of many students, who come to school dressed casually in jeans and Levis. Finally, he emphasized that proper attire creates a better climate for learning. This last point, Mr. Atkins stressed, is crucial in a school of declining standards.

PARAGRAPH 2: *Three important reasons for a dress code arranged in ascending order, the third one being the most important*

The interview lasted a half-hour, after which Mr. Atkins praised us for our interest and involvement. One week later, I read my report to other students.

PARAGRAPH 3: *Conclusion of interview and what took place after it*

Basic Components

This report on an interview with a school principal contains the following features:

Paragraph 1: Where the interview took place, its purpose, and some description of the principal.

Writing the Report

Paragraph 2: Three observations made by the writer, all arranged in *ascending order*, the last one being the most important.

Paragraph 3: The conclusion of the interview and what took place after it.

Evaluation

This report is outstanding because it

1. Uses all the notes given.
2. Presents key observations in *ascending order*, the most important being: "He finally emphasized that proper attire creates a better climate for learning."
3. Combines notes, such as: "The interview lasted a half-hour, after which Mr. Atkins praised us for our interest and involvement."
4. Develops certain notes further, such as: "At first, he discussed the need for a dress code, *pointing out how few rules and regulations are respected nowadays*," and "Second, he expressed his concern about the informality of many students, *who come to school dressed casually in jeans and Levis*.
5. Uses such transitionals as "at first," "second," "this last point."
6. Is free of major mechanical and grammatical errors.

FOLLOW-UP EXERCISE

In interviewing a person, you can record too much information, since your questions will often bring more than one response. Therefore, select three major areas that relate to the topic and arrange them in *ascending order*, reserving the most important for last.

Plan an interview with your principal concerning a major problem that affects many students. Ask questions that elicit reasons for a particular decision. Write those reasons down in the form of notes. Select three important ones and group them in *ascending order*. Then complete your report.

Writing the Report

Final Analysis

Write everything down at first, then make a decision. The decision should lead to an outline such as this:

Paragraph 1: Where the interview took place, its purpose, and a description of the person interviewed.

Paragraph 2: Three major observations about a changed plan, arranged in *ascending order*, the last one being the most important.

Paragraph 3: The conclusion of the interview and what followed.

Lesson 3

REPORTING ON A RALLY AGAINST THE DRAFT

THE WRITING TASK

A rally against a proposed draft for 18-year-olds is being held on a Saturday. You have been asked to attend as an observer and to report on the rally to a committee in your school. Your notes—shown in the box below—will be the basis for this school report.

NOTES ON A RALLY AGAINST THE DRAFT

We didn't get home till late
The rally lasted all day
Immediately, a fight broke out between supporters and opponents of the draft
Many in the crowd jeered the speakers
Others in the crowd cheered the speakers
The rally started about noon
Most of the crowd consisted of young people
The majority appeared to be against the draft

Writing the Report

> There were many speakers, both for and against
> One speaker received overwhelming applause
> The press was there to take pictures
> I saw several people I knew well

Arrange all these notes into one final written form. In your report, be certain to:

1. Arrange and develop all the notes.
2. Write complete sentences.
3. Edit your writing for correctness.

ANALYSIS OF THE TASK

What Are You Being Asked to Do?

Write a fully developed report on a rally against the draft, using the notes given, to be presented to a committee in school.

How to Respond

Study the notes carefully to place them in a certain order. In this case, group them in *descending order*: the most important thing that happened, a second important thing, a third important thing, etc.

THE MODEL

Report on a Rally Against the Draft

Combining notes

> The rally I attended, consisting mostly of young people, lasted all day, starting about noon. I noticed that the press was there to take pictures.

PARAGRAPH 1: *When the rally took place; who the people were*

Adding details

   Immediately, there was a fight between supporters and opponents of the draft. This was certainly the most important occurrence which I viewed. Prior to that, <u>names had been called, and a few members of the crowd had exchanged insults</u>. After the fight had been broken up, <u>Congressman Smith spoke</u>

PARAGRAPH 2: *Important highlights of the rally, arranged in descending order*

101

Adding details about the unfairness of the draft bill; he received overwhelming applause. With the majority appearing to be against the draft, many jeered those speaking for the bill and then cheered those speaking against it.

    I saw several familiar faces in the crowd. We discussed the rally briefly, and then I boarded the chartered bus back to our neighborhood.

PARAGRAPH 3: *Recognizing others, going home*

Basic Components

This report on a rally against the draft provides the following:

Paragraph 1: Details of when the rally started and who the people were.
Paragraph 2: Details of what took place, which are arranged in *descending order* of importance.
Paragraph 3: A brief conclusion.

Evaluation

The report is praiseworthy because it

1. Uses all the notes given.
2. Presents them in a logical order—the most important detail, a second important detail, a third, etc.
3. Combines notes into fuller sentences, such as: "The rally I attended, consisting mostly of young people, lasted all day, starting about noon," and "I noticed that the press was there to take pictures."
4. Adds words to flesh out details, such as: "names had been called, and a few members of the crowd had exchanged insults," and "We discussed the rally briefly, and then I boarded the chartered bus. . . ."
5. Uses transitionals to bridge details, such as: "immediately," "after the fight had been broken up," "with the majority appearing to be against the draft," "then."
6. Is free of major mechanical and grammatical errors.

Writing the Report

FOLLOW-UP EXERCISE

Rallies can be dramatic events. A lot happens when a big crowd assembles and many speakers give their ideas. Therefore, a report should contain only the most important happenings. One effective technique is to start with the most important one, then give the second, the third, and so on. This follows the *descending order* pattern.

Using this pattern, plan to attend the next meeting in your school or community if that deals with a major issue. Take notes as you listen, arrange them in *descending order*, and expand on the notes to produce a fully written report.

Final Analysis

As an observer taking notes on an important event, be sure to record details: the place of the meeting, the people involved, what the speakers say, the interaction of the crowd. Organize it all into a useful outline:

Paragraph 1: Where and when the meeting took place and who attended it.
Paragraph 2: Significant happenings—the most important one, another important one, a third, etc.
Paragraph 3: The conclusion of the meeting.

Lesson 4

REPORTING ON A MEETING WITH A STUDENT ORGANIZATION

THE WRITING TASK

You have been asked to attend a meeting of your high-school student council and report to the class about what happened. While you are at the meeting, you take notes of the proceedings. These notes are in the box below.

NOTES ON STUDENT COUNCIL MEETING

Meeting started late
President spoke first, then treasurer
New and old business
Problems of school discussed
Senior prom the major concern
Members of council differed on event
Meeting lasted two hours
Major concern finally resolved
Decision to report to principal and students

Writing the Report

Arrange all these notes into a final written form. In your report, be certain to:

1. Arrange and develop all the notes.
2. Write complete sentences.
3. Edit your writing for correctness.

ANALYSIS OF THE TASK

What Are You Being Asked to Do?

Write a fully developed report on a high-school student council meeting for your social studies class.

How to Respond

Look over all the notes carefully, fleshing them out with added details and further information. If necessary, rearrange them so that they fall into chronological order.

NOTES ON STUDENT COUNCIL MEETING [EXPANDED]

The student council meeting scheduled for 8 P.M. started at 8:30

The president spoke first, introducing new members; then the treasurer gave his budget report

New business was taken up, then old

Three important school matters were discussed

Whether to have a senior prom or not was the major concern

Some members argued for it, while others argued against it

The resolution was to have a senior prom

It was decided to report the resolution to the principal and students

The meeting lasted for two hours, from 8:30 to 10:30

Writing the Report

These notes have been arranged *chronologically* (as they actually happened). This enables the writer to ensure continuity in the report of the special occasion.

THE MODEL

Report on the Student Council Meeting

Transitionals

The student council meeting, scheduled for 8 P.M., started at 8:30. The president was the first to speak, highlighting goals for the year and introducing new members; <u>then</u> the treasurer gave his budget report on expenditures and membership dues. <u>Following that,</u> new business, such as approving new officers, was taken up, and old business, such as ratifying rules and regulations, was considered.

Of the three important school problems discussed--cutting policy, grading, and deciding whether to hold a senior prom--the matter of the senior prom became the major concern. <u>While</u> some members spoke openly about the advantages of ending the year with a happy event, others argued against it on the ground that it is too expensive and that many students cannot afford such an expense. <u>Finally,</u> on the basis of the vote taken, it was resolved to hold a senior prom on June 28. This decision is to be reported to the principal as well as the students.

<u>Altogether,</u> the meeting lasted for two hours, from 8:30 to 10:30, when the members adjourned.

PARAGRAPH 1: *Organizes details around what happened first— business matters (chronological)*

PARAGRAPH 2: *Organizes details around what happened next— discussion of problem (chronological)*

PARAGRAPH 3: *Closes the report with time ended*

Writing the Report

Evaluation

This above report is a good one because it

1. Organizes details *chronologically* (what happened first, second, etc.).
2. Is written factually (tells what really happened).
3. Is written objectively (without bias).
4. Is complete and unified.
5. Records significant proceedings.
6. Is free of major errors in the use of language.

FOLLOW-UP EXERCISE

Arrange to attend a student council meeting in your school. Listen and observe. Take notes on the proceedings, then rearrange and develop these notes into a full, *chronologically sequenced* report you can present to your teacher.

Final Analysis

When you report on any meeting, you will make a number of observations. Your job is to record what you consider to be the most important details. Setting them in *chronological order* is one effective way of doing it. A simple plan is as follows:

Paragraph 1: Where and when the meeting took place and who attended.
Paragraph 2: What happened first.
Details.
Paragraph 3: What happened second.
Details.
Paragraph 4: What happened next.
Details.
Paragraph 5: How the meeting was brought to a close.
Details.

Lesson 5

REPORTING ON A SCHOOL EVENT

THE WRITING TASK

A professional acting group has been invited to perform highlights from the play *Romeo and Juliet* at your school. As a reporter for the school newspaper, you have been assigned to attend the performance to take notes, for a possible newspaper article of what they do. Your notes are in the box below.

NOTES ON A SCHOOL EVENT

Arena Players sent a group of actors
The Observer, my school paper, sent me to gather notes
All junior classes came to the auditorium
Teachers were alerted in advance
Principal introduced the actors
They presented highlights of *Romeo and Juliet*
One of them gave us a short talk on the play
The actors were very animated
The audience appreciated the performance
The group stayed for the whole day
The audience was well-behaved

Writing the Report

> Questions were asked at the end
> One actor told us about his training
> We were told the group would return

Arrange all these notes into a final written form. In your report, be certain to:

1. Arrange and develop all the notes.
2. Write complete sentences.
3. Edit your writing for correctness.

ANALYSIS OF THE TASK

What Are You Being Asked to Do?

Write a fully developed report on a school event, specifically an acting performance put on by a visiting group, for your school newspaper.

How to Respond

Study the notes carefully to determine how they should be arranged *chronologically*. That is, regroup them according to when each event occurred. Expand on each note to make it a fully developed sentence.

THE MODEL

Report on a School Event

Appositives

The Observer, my school paper, sent me on an interesting assignment to gather notes on a special school performance. The Arena Players, a group of actors from a neighboring theater, had arranged to present highlights of the play Romeo and Juliet for all junior classes.

PARAGRAPH 1: *Centers details around reason for assignment*

Writing the Report

Complex sentences: linkage of two related ideas

<u>In advance of the players' arrival</u>, junior class teachers were alerted to ways of preparing students for the performance. After the principal introduced the actors, one of them gave us a short talk on the play—why and how it had been chosen. While the actors went through their lines, the audience was well-behaved and seemed to appreciate the performance, especially the animation of the actors.

PARAGRAPH 2: *Groups notes around the actors and their performance (chronological order)*

Prepositional phrase

<u>Toward the end,</u> one actor told us about his training and all the work that went into a performance. At the end, many questions were asked by the students, who wanted to know about the life of an actor and how a young person could begin his or her training. After the answers were given, the classes were summoned to their rooms, where they were told that the group of actors would return another day to present the highlights of a different play.

PARAGRAPH 3: *Focuses on the conclusion and its effects*

Relative clauses

Basic Components

This report on a school event contains the following:

Paragraph 1: A clear statement of the reason for the report—the event and the student's assignment.
Paragraph 2: Details of the performance as they occurred in time.
Paragraph 3: The conclusion of the event and its effect on the audience.

Evaluation

This report is well done because it

1. Organizes the notes given into three distinct paragraphs.
2. Arranges the notes given *chronologically*, showing details as they actually occurred.
3. Expands each note into a fully developed sentence.
4. Links notes together interestingly. For example, "after the principal introduced the actors, one of them gave us a short talk on the play—why and how it had been chosen" couples the two separate notes: "Principal introduced the actors" and "one of them gave us a short talk on the play."
5. Uses appositives to provide explanations, such as "*The Observer*, my school paper," and "The Arena Players, a group of actors from a neighboring theater" (Paragraph 1).
6. Uses prepositional phrases to show time, such as "in advance of the players' arrival"; adverbial clauses to show time, such as "after the principal introduced the actors" and "while the actors went through their lines" (Paragraph 2).

FOLLOW-UP EXERCISE

Think of a recent school event you attended, such as an athletic contest, a school play, or a trip to a famous place. List what you observed about the event. Then rearrange the list so that the details fall into place *chronologically*. Expand, rearrange, and develop these notes into a full, readable report.

Final Analysis

Any school event will present many details that can be recorded. It is your job to record those that are most important, leaving out the lesser ones. The idea is to present, in a *chronological pattern*, the highlights that will capture the attention of a reader who was not there. A simple plan to cover any event is:

Introductory Paragraph 1: The reason for the report and why you are there.

Main Paragraph 2: All the most important details woven together in order of occurrence (*chronologically*).

Writing the Report

	Details expanded, separated, or combined.
	Sentences written with appositives as well as adverbial phrases and clauses.
Concluding Paragraph 3:	How the event came to an end and affected the audience.

Lesson 6
REPORTING ON A SCHOOL BOARD MEETING

THE WRITING TASK

Your school board has scheduled a very important meeting on budget review. This meeting will determine whether the proposed budget will be accepted or rejected. As an officer of the student council, you have been asked to attend the meeting to take notes for a report to your organization. Your notes are in the box on the next page.

Writing the Report

> **NOTES ON THE SCHOOL BOARD MEETING**
>
> Budget items were explained line by line
> Meeting lasted three hours
> Many parents rose to protest cuts
> Meeting started promptly at 8:30
> President had to curb the noise
> Several parents supported cuts
> Agendas were given out at the beginning
> Board members gave their positions
> Declining enrollment was the issue
> The proposal for cutbacks was reviewed
> Some teachers and students were present
> There was a big turnout

Arrange all these notes into a final written form. In your report, be certain to:

1. Arrange and develop all the notes.
2. Write complete sentences.
3. Edit your writing for correctness.

ANALYSIS OF THE TASK

What Are You Being Asked to Do?

Write a fully developed report on a school board meeting for your student council.

How to Respond

Study the notes carefully to see how they are arranged. Regroup them *chronologically*. Where you can, expand on each note to make it a fully developed, more interesting sentence.

Writing the Report

THE MODEL

Report on a School Board Meeting

Prepositional phrase

Adverbial clause

Adjectival clause

I attended an important school board meeting on proposed budgetary cuts. When I arrived, shortly before it started, I noticed a big turnout. At 8:30 promptly, the meeting started with the distribution of agendas.

At first, the board members gave their positions on reasons for the proposed cuts. After they dealt with the issue of declining enrollment, the President had to curb the noise that resulted when many parents rose to protest the cuts. After the noise had subsided, other parents rose to support the cuts. There seemed to be a balance of pros and cons regarding the main issue.

Looking around, I noticed some teachers and students present, all of them listening intently. Later, when the proposal for cutbacks was fully reviewed, the meeting, which lasted three hours, was called to a close by the president.

PARAGRAPH 1: *Groups notes around the beginning of the meeting*

PARAGRAPH 2: *Arranges details around the issues and their effect on the audience (chronological order)*

PARAGRAPH 3: *Sets notes around final phase of the meeting*

Basic Components

The above report on a community event contains the following:

Sentence 1: A clear statement as to the importance of the meeting.
Sentences 2–7: Details of the major events of the meeting, all arranged *chronologically*, in order of their occurrence.
Sentence 8: Final statement on the close of the meeting.

Evaluation

This report is commendable because it

1. Organizes the notes in a logical pattern.
2. Uses all the notes given.
3. Expands and develops individual sentences to make them more interesting.
4. Uses time-linking words, such as "at first," "later."
5. Uses prepositional phrases to show time connections, such as "at 8:30 promptly," and a variety of clauses, such as "when I arrived shortly before it started," "after they dealt with the issue of declining enrollment," and "after the noise had subsided."
6. Uses adjectival clauses, such as "which lasted three hours."
7. Combines two notes into one sentence: "I attended an important school board meeting on proposed budgetary cuts."

FOLLOW-UP EXERCISE

Inquire as to the next meeting of your local school board. Attend the meeting and think of yourself as an objective observer. List what you consider to be the major highlights. Then rearrange your notes so that they follow one another *chronologically*. Expand and develop these notes into a full, readable report.

Final Analysis

At any community meeting for large numbers of people, there will probably be a great number of details to be noted. Good reporting requires a selection of only the most important ones—arranged as they happened, *chronologically*—to give the reader a clear idea of what occurred. A simple plan for a one-paragraph report is:

Sentence 1:	A clear statement of the meeting's purpose and importance.
Middle sentences:	Major details of the meeting, all arranged *chronologically*, in the order of occurrence.
Final sentence:	Wrap-up statement on the close of the meeting—when, how, and final decision.

Lesson 7

REPORTING ON A TRIP

THE WRITING TASK

You accompany your class on a school trip to a natural history museum. Your teacher has requested that you take notes of the exhibits you see as you stroll about. These notes will provide the basis for a report you will give in class. Your notes are in the box below.

> **NOTES ON OUR SCHOOL TRIP**
>
> This natural history museum is fantastic
> We had a lot of fun and learned a lot
> At the end of the day, I was sorry it was over
> Our teacher, Mr. Jones, was with us all the time
> The afternoon was spent in the Hall of Evolution
> Lunch was at twelve in the cafeteria
> There were many other school groups
> We ate sandwiches and bought sodas
> There was a short break, outside, after lunch
> During the morning we were given a general orientation
> Special guides were provided
> The dinosaurs were the greatest sight

Writing the Report

Arrange all these notes into a final written form. In your report, be certain to:

1. Arrange and develop all notes.
2. Write complete sentences.
3. Edit your writing for correctness.

ANALYSIS OF THE TASK

What Are You Being Asked to Do?

Write a fully developed report on a school trip, to be presented in class, using the notes given.

How to Respond

Study the notes carefully to determine how they should be rearranged. Regroup them according to when each event actually occurred. That is, aim for a *chronological arrangement*. Where possible, expand further on any notes, but be sure your sentence structure is sound.

THE MODEL

Report on a School Trip

The natural history museum I visited with my class was not only fun but also gave us a fantastic learning experience. Accompanied by Mr. Jones, our teacher, we arrived early in the morning, when we were given a general orientation by one of the museum officials. After that, a special guide took us to observe the more popular halls. While we walked from one hall to another, I noticed many other school groups. The highlight of the morning tour was the dinosaurs, which were the most memorable sight.

Sentence variety

Adverbial clause

Adjectival clause

PARAGRAPH 1: *Arranges details on morning activities chronologically*

Writing the Report

Prepositional phrase

<u>At twelve</u>, we ate lunch in the cafeteria. We sat around gobbling sandwiches and sipping sodas. Then we took a short break outside, to get some air and to exercise our muscles. The break prepared us for the next part.

    The afternoon was spent in the Hall of Evolution, where we studied early human beings and their development into today's human beings. Our guide pointed out important exhibits that gave us a good understanding of the subject. Mr. Jones was helpful as well. The museum trip was so rewarding that, at the end of the day, I was sorry it was over.

PARAGRAPH 2: *Organizes notes dealing with lunch and a break*

PARAGRAPH 3: *Structures notes around afternoon activities chronologically*

Basic Components

This report on a school trip tells about the following:

Paragraph 1:   What happened in the morning.
Paragraph 2:   The lunch break.
Paragraph 3:   What happened in the afternoon.

    Dividing the report in this manner—what happened in the morning, during lunch, in the afternoon—structures the events *chronologically*. This is a very good way of preparing a report.

Evaluation

This report is commendable because it

1. Uses all the notes given.
2. Presents them in order of occurrence.
3. Expands certain notes to add interest and create variety. For example, Paragraph 3 includes more information to round out the experience.
4. Structures all notes into a variety of sound sentences. For ex-

ample, in Paragraph 1 the sentence "accompanied by Mr. Jones, our teacher, we arrived early in the morning, when we were given a general orientation by one of the museum officials" combines three separate ideas into one sentence unit.
5. Uses prepositional constructions such as "at twelve."
6. Uses adjectival constructions such as "which were the most memorable sight," and "that gave us a good understanding of the subject."

FOLLOW-UP EXERCISE

The events of school trips are easily recorded in the order in which they happened. The *chronological arrangement*, therefore, is the easiest way to group your notes. But there are also other ways to prepare reports, as we will see later.

In any case, think of your last school trip. Write down a dozen happenings you can recall. Then rearrange these notes *chronologically*. When you have done this, decide which of them should be expanded into fuller ideas.

Final Analysis

The key to good reporting is focusing on the essentials. Therefore, always write about the most important happenings and leave the lesser ones out. In this way, you will produce a more interesting report that will engage your listeners. A simple preparatory outline can serve well.

Paragraph 1: What happened in the first part of the trip.
Paragraph 2: What happened next—lunch or a break.
Paragraph 3: What happened at the end of the day.

Lesson 8

REPORTING ON CONDITIONS IN A LOCAL HOSPITAL

THE WRITING TASK

As part of your project on community services, you decide to visit a local hospital to study the quality of care received by the patients. You visit a number of patients to find out how they feel about the conditions and how well the staff cares for them. You take notes on your observations. These notes will be the basis of a report to be given later in class. Your notes are in the box on the next page.

Writing the Report

> **NOTES ON PATIENT CARE
> IN A LOCAL HOSPITAL**
>
> I talked with six patients
> I visited Smith General Hospital for one day
> I left the hospital feeling discouraged
> It was obvious that the majority of patients felt they were not well treated
> Nurses did not always come when called
> Doctors tended to come infrequently
> Meals were considered unappealing
> Relatives did not visit patients often enough
> Mrs. Smith, an elderly woman, felt her family had abandoned her
> Mr. Jeremy complained about not getting the services he wanted
> One nurse insisted she could not get around to all patients
> I went with the purpose of seeing whether patients were satisfied with conditions

Arrange these notes into a final written form. In your report, be certain to:

1. Arrange and develop all notes.
2. Write complete sentences.
3. Edit your writing for correctness.

ANALYSIS OF THE TASK

What Are You Being Asked to Do?

Write a fully developed report on a visit to a local hospital to observe conditions of patient care, using the notes given.

How to Respond

Study the notes carefully to determine the best arrangement. Regroup them according to a logical pattern. Where possible, expand further on any of the notes.

Writing the Report

THE MODEL
Report on Patient Care in a Local Hospital

Combining notes

In order to see whether patients were satisfied with hospital conditions, I visited Smith General Hospital for one day. I planned to speak with a number of patients about services.

PARAGRAPH 1: *The purpose of visiting the hospital*

I was told, for one thing, that nurses were not always available when called. This resulted in complaints about lack of proper mail delivery, punctual meal service, and regularity of medication. When I asked a nurse about this matter, she told me that she could not always get around to all patients.

PARAGRAPH 2: *Unavailability of nurses caused complaints*

Parenthetical expressions

Another observation I made was that doctors tended to come infrequently. This made the patients irritable. Mr. Jeremy, in particular, complained about not getting the medical services he wanted.

PARAGRAPH 3: *Infrequent doctor visits caused patients to be irritable*

Expanding on notes

All the patients mentioned that the meals were unappealing. They called for a more varied menu and better-prepared food. The meals they received tended to depress their appetites.

PARAGRAPH 4: *Unappealing meals caused a loss of appetite*

Most of the patients, unfortunately, expressed a concern about relatives who did not visit them often enough. This lack made them feel sad and lonely. Mrs. Smith, an elderly woman, felt that her family had abandoned her.

PARAGRAPH 5: *Lack of visits from relatives caused loneliness and a feeling of abandonment*

After the visit, I left the hospital feeling discouraged, for it was obvious that the majority of patients felt that they were not being treated well. Apparently, many conditions at Smith General Hospital are causing pain and distress.

PARAGRAPH 6: *The writer's conclusion about patient care (effect)*

Basic Components

This report on patient care in a local hospital contains the following:

Paragraph 1: The purpose of visiting the hospital.
Paragraph 2: How the scarcity of nursing services caused complaints.
Paragraph 3: How the infrequency of doctor visits caused annoyance.
Paragraph 4: How the unappealing meals reduced patients' appetites.
Paragraph 5: How the lack of visits by relatives created a feeling of abandonment.
Paragraph 6: The writer's conclusion about what she saw about the level of patient care.

Evaluation

This report is praiseworthy because it

1. Uses all the notes given.
2. Highlights four important conditions.
3. Shows how these conditions affect the patients, using a *cause-effect* pattern.
4. Employs a variety of sentence types to make the report more interesting to read.
5. Expands on certain notes to give a fuller picture of the conditions: "All the patients mentioned that the meals were unappealing. They called for a more varied menu and better-prepared food. The meals they received tended to depress their appetites."
6. Uses parenthetical expressions to intensify the effect: "for one thing," "in particular," "unfortunately," "apparently."
7. Combines notes to show a relationship: "In order to see whether patients were satisfied with hospital conditions, I visited Smith General Hospital for one day. I planned to speak with a number of patients about services."
8. Is free of major mechanical and grammatical errors.

Writing the Report

FOLLOW-UP EXERCISE

Visit your local library to observe the conditions and how they affect the community. Speak to people in the library and ask them how satisfied they are. The basic question to use is, "How do you feel about this?" Then decide which three or four conditions are significant enough to write about.

Arrange these notes in a *cause-effect pattern*, expand on some, combine others, and complete your final report.

Final Analysis

You have to make a decision in this kind of report—that is, which conditions affect the most people? When you have decided this, you will be ready to structure your notes as follows:

Paragraph 1: The purpose of your visit.
Paragraph 2: One condition and its effect.
Paragraph 3: A second condition and its effect.
Paragraph 4: A third condition and its effect.
Paragraph 5: A fourth condition and its effect.
Paragraph 6: Your conclusion based on the observations you have made.

Lesson 9

REPORTING ON AN ATHLETIC MEET IN ANOTHER SCHOOL

THE WRITING TASK

As the sports reporter of your school newspaper, you are sent to another school to watch a rival basketball team play. The objective of your assignment is to compare the rival basketball team with your school team. The notes you take will be the basis of this comparison. These notes are in the box on the next page.

Writing the Report

> **NOTES ON AN ATHLETIC MEET IN ANOTHER SCHOOL**
>
> The Adams team played well most of the evening
> They play well together, show teamwork
> The team received a lot of support from students and cheerleaders
> They play a structured defense, averting many baskets
> Their coach pulls out players for the slightest reason
> They employ a snappy offense, according to plan
> Their star player, Jim Hoskins, is accurate 70% of the time
> They never give up, even when behind
> The final score was Adams, 98; opposing team, 79
> They have distinct advantages over our team at Kennedy
> They pass the ball frequently and thus wear their opponents down

Arrange all these notes in final written form. In your report, be certain to:

1. Arrange and develop all notes.
2. Write complete sentences.
3. Edit your writing for correctness.

ANALYSIS OF THE TASK

What Are You Being Asked to Do?

Write a fully developed report comparing a rival basketball team to your school team.

How to Respond

Study the notes carefully to review your observations of the rival basketball team. Then determine whether your school team com-

Writing the Report

pares well in every way. Remember: *a comparison may reveal similarities or differences.*

THE MODEL

Report on an Athletic Meet in Another School

I went to watch the Adams basketball team play last Friday night in their own school. My purpose was to compare them to our team, to predict how well we will do when we meet them in our own school.

In particular, their star player, Jim Hoskins, is accurate in his shots only 70% of the time, *while* our star, Billy Bold, scores 80% of the time. *Measured against* the poor attendance we get at our games, the Adams team receives a lot of support from students and cheerleaders. *Since* both teams employ a highscoring offense, it will be interesting to see which one succeeds. *Though* they play a structured defense, averting many baskets, our defense is tighter. *Since* they pass the ball frequently and thus wear their opponents down, we will have a hard time breaking through. Their coach pulls out players for the slightest reason, *while* ours keeps them in longer. *Unlike* our team, they play well together and show excellent teamwork.

The Adams team played well most of the evening. The final score was Adams, 98; opposing team, 79. My conclusion is that they have a distinct advantage over our team.

Comparative words

PARAGRAPH 1: *The purpose of watching a rival team play*

PARAGRAPH 2: *Comparisons of the Adams and Kennedy teams—superior and inferior qualities*

PARAGRAPH 3: *Observation and conclusion concerning the Adams team*

Writing the Report

Basic Components

This report on the two teams is commendable because it breaks down as follows:

Paragraph 1: The purpose of the visit to another school: to watch a rival team in action.
Paragraph 2: *Comparisons* made, both superior and inferior qualities.
Paragraph 3: A general observation of the Adams team and a conclusion as to their superiority.

Evaluation

This report features the following:

1. All the notes given are used.
2. The notes are used to compare important qualities of both teams.
3. Both superior and inferior qualities are indicated.
4. Comparative words are used to highlight playing qualities, such as: "since they pass the ball frequently and thus wear their opponents down, we will have a hard time breaking through" (superior quality), and "their coach pulls players out for the slightest reason, while ours keeps them in longer" (inferior quality).
5. A variety of complex sentences gives a clear picture of *comparative points*. For example, "Measured against the poor attendance we get at our games, the Adams team receives a lot of support from students and cheerleaders."
6. The writing is free of major mechanical and grammatical errors.

FOLLOW-UP EXERCISE

When you compare any team to another, you will observe both good and bad points. Weighing them all, you have to make a decision as to the ultimate advantages of one over the other. Plan to attend a sports competition between one of your school teams and a rival team. Write down what you see as good and bad points. Discuss each one in relation to both teams, then draw a conclusion as to which one, on the basis of observations, compares more favorably.

Final Analysis

When you make a *comparison*, you are looking for both similarities and dissimilarities. One, though, will outweigh the other on an overall basis. Therefore, although you are analyzing both similarities and dissimilarities in comparing two teams, the final decision as to which one is superior must depend on the number of careful observations you have made. A good report based on a comparison can accomplish this successfully.

Lesson 10

REPORTING ON A FRIEND'S SCHOOL PROM

THE WRITING TASK

One week after your own school prom, you are invited to a friend's prom in another school. While there, you notice many unique differences between the two proms. You jot these differences down as notes, which you will later discuss with your friend. Your notes are in the box on the next page.

Writing the Report

> **NOTES ON A FRIEND'S SCHOOL PROM**
>
> The Shoreham Manor, the place where the prom was held, was very formal
> The band played rock music all night
> There were about 200 couples
> The affair lasted until three in the morning
> The food was poorly prepared, very ordinary
> Groups of students banded together and didn't mix with others
> There were many speeches by student leaders
> Apparently, few teachers and their wives attended
> The cost was $60 per couple; at our prom, it was only $40
> There was no entertainment, only music
> Many students left early

Arrange all these notes into a final written report. In your report, be certain to:

1. Arrange and develop all notes.
2. Write complete sentences.
3. Edit your writing for correctness.

ANALYSIS OF THE TASK

What Are You Being Asked to Do?

Write a fully developed report, using the notes given, on a friend's school prom. This report is to be discussed with your friend later.

How to Respond

Study the notes carefully to determine how each one *contrasts* with a comparable quality of your own prom. Remember, you are contrasting: showing differences or dissimilarities. Where possible, expand further on any notes, but be sure your sentence structure is perfect.

Writing the Report

THE MODEL

Report on a Friend's School Prom

Combining notes

Having recently gone to my own school prom, I was invited to join my friend at his. The Shoreham Manor, the place where the prom was held, was very formal. The affair lasted until three in the morning, though many students left early. Altogether, there were about 200 couples present.

PARAGRAPH 1: *Where the prom was held and the number attending*

Contrasting words

The band played rock music all night, but there was no entertainment, while the band at our prom played only at intervals. Groups of students banded together and didn't mix with others; by comparison, our prom had a social and friendly atmosphere. At our prom, many teachers and their wives attended but there were few at my friend's. There were more speeches by student leaders here than we had had. Our cost of $40 per couple was far less than the $60 at the Shoreham. The food was poorly prepared, very ordinary, while our meal was delicious and inviting.

PARAGRAPH 2: *Six obvious differences between the two proms, all shown as contrasts*

In all, there were distinct differences between my friend's prom at the Shoreham Manor and my own.

PARAGRAPH 3: *Concluding observation on general differences*

Basic Components

This report on a friend's prom includes the following:

Paragraph 1: Facts about the prom.
Paragraph 2: Six obvious differences between the friend's prom and the writer's.
Paragraph 3: A concluding observation on general differences.

NOTE: While there may have been similarities, the writer has focused only on differences, fulfilling the purpose of the report.

Evaluation

This report is excellent because it

1. Uses all the notes given.
2. Presents them in a *contrast pattern*.
3. Combines notes, as in "The affair lasted until three in the morning, though many students left early."
4. Highlights contrasts with key words, such as "while," "by comparison," "but," "more . . . than," "far less than."
5. Structures sentences well. For example, "Having recently gone to my own school prom, I was invited to join my friend at his."
6. Is free of major mechanical and grammatical errors.

FOLLOW-UP EXERCISE

Think of two events that have sharp contrasts. They may be trips, proms, athletic events, shows, or talks by visitors. Jot down what these *contrasts* or differences are. Then, using contrast words to bridge your observations, flesh out your notes and write a complete report.

Final Analysis

While a comparison of two events may include both similar and dissimilar qualities, a *contrast* must be consistent in underscoring what is different. Usually, the purpose is to show to what degree one event is better than another. Simply, a structure of the following will work in just about all contrasts:

Paragraph 1: Description of the event being observed for a contrast with a previous one.
Paragraph 2: At least three apparent differences that set off one against the other.
Paragraph 3: A concluding statement as to which event is superior to the other.

Lesson 11

REPORTING ON A LIVE TELEVISION PROGRAM

THE WRITING TASK

You have received two tickets for the television program *The Dating Game*. Since you have never been to a television studio before, you take a notebook along in order to jot down your observations of what a live television program is like. These notes will be the basis of a report you give in class. Your notes are in the box on the next page.

Writing the Report

NOTES ON A LIVE TELEVISION PROGRAM

We were in the studio for a full hour
The program lasted exactly 30 minutes
There were four cameras around the stage
Contestants were summoned from the audience
Technicians controlled lighting and sound
The M.C. was prompted from behind the camera
Questions were flashed on big boards
Signs with the word "Applause" were held up
Prizes were neatly stacked in wings
The musicians played on the side
Watching it live is different from watching it at home

Arrange all these notes into a final written report. In your report, be certain to:

1. Arrange and develop all notes.
2. Write complete sentences.
3. Edit your writing for correctness.

ANALYSIS OF THE TASK

What Are You Being Asked to Do?

Write a fully developed report, using the notes given, on a live television program. You will later present this report in class.

How to Respond

Study your notes to determine a logical order. Regroup them in *spatial order*. Where possible, expand further on any notes, but be sure your sentence structure is sound.

Writing the Report

THE MODEL

Report on a Live Television Program

Adding key words

Watching a television program live is <u>certainly</u> different from watching it at home. At least, that is what I felt when a friend and I sat in the studio for a full hour, watching a 30-minute program called The Dating Game.

<u>Immediately,</u> I noticed many technicians controlling lighting and sound. There were four cameras around the stage. <u>As the program proceeded,</u> the musicians played on the side. <u>At different points,</u> signs with the word "Applause" were held up. <u>Contrary to what I thought,</u> the M.C. was prompted from behind the camera. <u>Also,</u> contestants were pre-selected and then summoned from the audience. Prizes for the winners were neatly stacked in the wings, each one tagged and ready for selection. <u>Though the M.C. asked the questions,</u> they were flashed on big boards out of camera range.

You notice a lot more detail in a studio than you can possibly see on your screen.

PARAGRAPH 1:
The differences between live and televised programs

PARAGRAPH 2:
A variety of details observed, all arranged spatially

PARAGRAPH 3:
Concluding generalization

Basic Components

This report on a live television program contains the following:

Paragraph 1: Establishes the differences between a live and a televised program.
Paragraph 2: Describes a variety of details inherent in the live program, all arranged *spatially*.
Paragraph 3: States a concluding generalization.

NOTE: A *spatial arrangement* is a listing of what the observer sees around him. The details are physical—in this case, technical features of the program. They should be presented in some logical progression: left to right, near to far, etc.

Evaluation

This report is commendable because it

1. Uses all the notes given.
2. Presents them in *spatial order*.
3. Expands on certain notes to give a clearer picture—for example, "Prizes for the winners were neatly stacked in the wings, each one tagged and ready for selection."
4. Includes key words to intensify or emphasize a quality—for example, "certainly," "immediately," "as the program proceeded," "at different points," "contrary to what I thought," "also," "though the M.C. asked the questions."
5. Contains variety of sentence structure.
6. Is free of major mechanical and grammatical errors.

FOLLOW-UP EXERCISE

People often describe situations or scenes *spatially*. This arrangement requires the ability to look around and pick out distinctive things to emphasize.

Select a place of entertainment you know well, such as a theater, a movie house, a sports arena. Look around carefully and record obvious physical features. Then rearrange these notes in a satisfying order and write a fully developed report.

Final Analysis

Rely on your powers of observation in reporting *spatially*. Look, see, study, and record everything; then make a decision as to which observations you will use in the report. A helpful outline will be:

Paragraph 1: A general description of the place you are observing.
Paragraph 2: Distinctive features of the place.
Paragraph 3: A concluding generalization about the place or a comparison to another like it.

Lesson 12

REPORTING ON A NATURE-STUDY TRIP

THE WRITING TASK

You accompany your science class on a nature-study trip. The purpose is to observe, record, and write about an arboretum. These notes will be the basis of a report you give later in class. Your notes are in the box below.

NOTES ON A NATURE-STUDY TRIP

We stayed the whole day, observing and talking
The Cutting Arboretum preserves natural beauty
It is open from 9 A.M. to 5 P.M.
Trees of all kinds abound on the site
Red and black wildflowers grow near the stream
There are many paths through the woods
A guide escorted us to explain flora
Birds of different species nest in the trees
We asked our guide many questions
Small animals make their homes in the woods
The leaves had fallen to the ground
I went with my science class to study nature

Writing the Report

Arrange all these notes into a final written form. In your report, be certain to:

1. Arrange and develop all notes.
2. Write complete sentences.
3. Edit your writing for correctness.

ANALYSIS OF THE TASK

What Are You Being Asked to Do?

Write a fully developed report, using the notes given, on a nature-study trip to an arboretum. Your report is to be presented in a science class later.

How to Respond

Study the notes carefully to determine a logical order. In this case, think of a *spatial arrangement*, describing details as you see them around you. Where possible, expand further on any notes, but be sure your sentence structure is sound.

THE MODEL

Report on a Nature-Study Trip

Expanding notes

I went with my science class to study nature in a beautiful place. The Cutting Arboretum, open from 9 A.M. to 5 P.M., preserves natural beauty.

A guide escorted us to explain the flora found there. She pointed to several types and gave us their names. All around us, the leaves had fallen to the ground.

Combining notes

We walked along the many paths through the woods to sight birds of different species that nest in the trees. Trees of all kinds abound on the site, as well as red and black wildflowers growing near the stream. We

PARAGRAPH 1: *The place visited and the purpose in going*

PARAGRAPH 2: *Distinctive details observed, arranged spatially, as the writer sees them*

```
noticed small animals making their
homes in the woods.
    We asked our guide many questions,
which she answered very graciously. We
stayed all day, observing and talking
about what we saw. It was a rare
opportunity to observe nature in its
simple but beautiful forms.
```

PARAGRAPH 3:
The time spent at the place and the writer's concluding summation

Basic Components

This report on a nature-study trip contains the following:

Paragraph 1: A general description of the place visited and the purpose of the visit.
Paragraph 2: Distinctive details observed *spatially*, as the writer sees them.
Paragraph 3: The writer's concluding summation about the place visited.

NOTE: A *spatial arrangement* includes physical features characteristic of the place being observed, arranged naturally and in an orderly manner.

Evaluation

This report is commendable because it

1. Uses all the notes given.
2. Presents them as the writer sees the sharp details around him.
3. Expands certain notes to round out a detail, such as, "A guide escorted us to explain the flora found there. She pointed to several types and gave us their names."
4. Combines certain notes to improve sentence structure, such as, "The Cutting Arboretum, open from 9 A.M. to 5 P.M., preserves natural beauty."
5. Uses prepositional phrases to indicate *where*, such as, "in a beautiful place," "all around us," "on the site," "in the woods."
6. Adds a closing summation: "It was a rare opportunity to observe nature in its simple but beautiful forms."
7. Is free of major mechanical and grammatical errors.

Writing the Report

FOLLOW-UP EXERCISE

Select any outdoor place that you find interesting. Visit this place to observe distinctive qualities that you can actually see, smell, and touch. Record your observations as notes, *spatially*. Then rearrange them in the best order possible for a fully developed report.

Final Analysis

Studying the outdoors, a nature site, offers many possibilities for observation. Since there are so many details to note, it is wise to select only the most important ones—those that stand out. When you have decided on from three to five such details, you can write your report according to this outline:

Paragraph 1: The place you visited and your purpose in going there.
Paragraph 2: Three to five physically distinctive details about the place.
Paragraph 3: A concluding statement that sums up the experience of the trip.

CONCLUSION TO CHAPTER ON REPORT WRITING

In this chapter, you have learned that writing a report is a task that requires organization and precision. Organization refers to the way you arrange your notes. Precision refers to the language you use to express and expand these notes into sentences and paragraphs.

Remember, a report is a record of an event that has already happened. As the writer, it is your job to study the notes you have taken to decide how they should be organized. Depending on the event, they can be organized (1) chronologically, (2) by contrast and comparison, (3) spatially, (4) by cause and effect, (5) in descending order of importance, or (6) in ascending order of importance.

6

WRITING THE PERSUASIVE COMPOSITION

Think of how many times you have tried to persuade others of your opinion, of your desire to go to a particular place, of your position on some important issue. In speaking, we do this easily enough; but in writing we are forced to be organized, convincing, and as factual as possible.

Therefore, the purpose of this section of the book is to show you, by application and example, those skills that you will need to perform well on the Regents Competency Test question which deals with persuasive writing.

Simply put, all persuasive writing has a similar format:

Writing the Persuasive Composition

MODEL
Persuasive Writing

Paragraph 1: *Your opinion or position.*
Paragraph 2: *Reason 1.*
Supporting details.
Paragraph 3: *Reason 2.*
Supporting details.
Paragraph 4: *Reason 3.*
Supporting details.
Paragraph 5: *Concluding statement* of original opinion or position.

NOTE: This chapter will show you how to arrange your reasons and details by *ascending order, chronological order, descending order, cause and effect,* and *comparison and contrast.*

PERSUASIVE COMPOSITION CHECKLIST

Content

1. A clear, direct, convincing statement of your position.
2. Clearly thought-out reasons why you are taking this position.
3. Explanations, or development, of these reasons.
4. A concluding statement of your position that relates to the opening statement.

Organization

1. Your specific position and why you hold it.
2. Supporting reasons that deepen your position and make it convincing.
3. Your suggestion of the solution to the particular problem you are writing about.

Arrangement

1. **Chronological order:** a time order in which your reasons are rooted—which reason occurred first, which second, which third, etc.

Writing the Persuasive Composition

2. **Contrast and comparison:** Relating your position to an opposite one or to a similar one.
3. **Cause and effect:** Showing how the problem is affecting others.
4. **Ascending order:** listing your reasons in an order of importance—one important reason, a second important reason, and the most important reason.
5. **Descending order:** Listing your reasons in an order of importance—the most important reason, another important reason, a third important reason.

THINKING THROUGH YOUR POSITION AND REASONS

Now study the following issues and decide what your position statement would be, along with supporting reasons. Decide which order of importance you will use: descending or ascending.

Situation 1: You believe the government is spending too much money on national defense.
Position statement _____
 Reason 1: _____
 Reason 2: _____
 Reason 3: _____

Situation 2: You are against further budget cuts in your school district.
Position statement _____
 Reason 1: _____
 Reason 2: _____
 Reason 3: _____

Situation 3: You are for a national health plan that would guarantee medical care for everyone.
Position statement _____
 Reason 1: _____
 Reason 2: _____
 Reason 3: _____

Lesson 1

PERSUADING A SCHOOL PRINCIPAL TO DROP A SUBJECT FROM THE CURRICULUM

THE WRITING TASK

You have been asked by your principal to submit to him your comments about courses in the school. The purpose of this request is to have the student body indicate courses they like and those they don't. Write a composition of about 150 words convincing your principal that a particular subject should be dropped from the school curriculum.

Writing the Persuasive Composition

ANALYSIS OF THE TASK

What Are You Being Asked to Do?

Write 150 words supporting your position that a course you are taking be dropped.

How to Respond

First, think of the course and how you feel about it. Then think of three convincing reasons why it should be dropped. Outline as follows:

Paragraph 1: Position or opinion about the course.
Paragraph 2: First important reason why it should be dropped.
Paragraph 3: Second reason why it should be dropped.
Paragraph 4: Third and most important reason why it should be dropped.
Paragraph 5: Restatement of original position.

THE MODEL

Reasons Why a Course Should Be Dropped

It is my firm opinion that algebra, one of the courses given at Southside High School, is useless for most students and therefore should be eliminated from the school program.

One important reason for this opinion is that studying algebra is irrelevant to my life. In no way do I see how this subject will be of help in the job I get when I leave school. How can computing the speed of a train be of any benefit to me in the work world?

My second reason is that algebra is a difficult course that many students fail. Because of the teachers and what they demand, because of the topics that have to be learned, too many students either fail or receive low marks.

| Sentence variety |

PARAGRAPH 1: *States the writer's position on dropping a course*

PARAGRAPH 2: *Presents one important reason to support position, and develops it*

PARAGRAPH 3: *Presents the second important reason to support position, and develops it*

Writing the Persuasive Composition

Sentence variety

My third and most important reason is that the time spent mastering algebraic equations could be better used studying other courses, such as driver education, biology, or computer science. Compared to these subjects, algebra has no practical value.

In conclusion, since many students feel as I do--that algebra is irrelevant, difficult, and wasteful--it would be wise to eliminate it from Southside's curriculum.

PARAGRAPH 4: *Presents the most important reason to support position, and develops it (ascending order)*

PARAGRAPH 5: **Summarizes** *all reasons in a concluding statement*

Basic Components

The above persuasive composition on convincing a school principal to drop a subject contains the following:

Paragraph 1: The writer's position that a math course is useless.
Paragraph 2: The irrelevancy of algebra to real life.
Paragraph 3: The difficulty of algebra for many students.
Paragraph 4: The need to spend more time mastering other subjects.
Paragraph 5: A conclusion that algebra should be eliminated from the curriculum.

Evaluation

This persuasive composition is commendable because it

1. States a clear position and supports it with reasons.
2. Presents the reasons convincingly, in *ascending order* (first important reason, second reason, third and most important reason).
3. Utilizes a variety of sentence structure.
4. Is paragraphed logically—position, reasons, conclusion.

FOLLOW-UP EXERCISE

Think of all the subjects you are taking in your school and decide which one you honestly feel should be eliminated from the school program. Write a persuasive paper to your principal in which you (1) state and qualify your position, (2) defend that position with three reasons in ascending order, and (3) conclude with a restatement of the same position.

Final Analysis

A persuasive composition has only one purpose: to convince your reader that your position is a valid one. Whatever you may be arguing about, the format of your writing should always be as follows:

Paragraph 1: A clear, direct statement of your position.
Paragraph 2: The first reason and an explanation of it.
Paragraph 3: The second important reason plus explanation.
Paragraph 4: The third most important reason and explanation.
Paragraph 5: The concluding statement in which you reaffirm your original position.

Lesson 2

PERSUADING A TEACHER TO CHANGE A MARK

THE WRITING TASK

Your English teacher has given you a final grade of 75. You are disappointed because you think you deserve an 85. When you speak to him about the matter, he tells you to put it into writing for his consideration. Write a composition of about 150 words persuading your English teacher that the mark of 75 should be changed to 85.

ANALYSIS OF THE TASK

What Are You Being Asked to Do?

Put into writing your main reasons for feeling that your work deserves a higher grade.

How to Respond

Consider all the reasons you have supporting your position that you deserve an 85. Outline them first, as follows:

Reason 1: I have taken all tests and handed in all reports.
Reason 2: I have been present in class every day.
Reason 3: All homework assignments but two were completed.

Now look at your reasons to determine which is most important. Rearrange your outline to fit the pattern of *ascending order*, as follows:

Reason 1: I have been present in class every day.
Reason 2: All homework assignments but two were completed.
Reason 3: I have taken all tests and handed in all reports.

By using *ascending order*, you have saved your most important reason for last, providing a strong finish to your persuasive paper. With the outline as it is, you can add your introductory and concluding parts.

THE MODEL

Reasons Why My Grade Should Be Higher

My final grade in English is definitely unfair and invalid. As I view my record in your class for the semester, I am convinced that I deserve an 85, not the 75 you gave me on the report card.

Transition

To begin with, my attendance record is a good one. I was present in class every day and, as a result, have not missed any work. My notes are up to date with regard to the work covered during the period. Certainly, a consistent attendance record is an important factor.

Simple sentence

PARAGRAPH 1: *Writer establishes purpose—to protest unfairness of mark*

PARAGRAPH 2: *Writer offers first reason—good attendance record*

Writing the Persuasive Composition

Transition — Also, except for two assignments, all required homework was completed. Your record should indicate checks for the times they were collected and turned back. Your initials on the top of each one proves they were satisfactory. If you wish, I can show them to you, as I have saved all the papers. That, too, is to my credit.

PARAGRAPH 3: *Writer offers second reason—completion of homework*

Finally and most important, I have taken all tests and turned in all reports. My high grades on the midterm as well as the final, in addition to superior grades on the three book reports, are proof of my enthusiasm and dedication to my studies. Since major tests and book reports comprise 50% of the final grade, I do not understand why I have been penalized.

PARAGRAPH 4: *Writer stresses* most important *reason—high grades on tests and reports (ascending order)*

Complex sentence — In short, I contend, for all these reasons, that you erred in determining my final grade. I wish, therefore, to review my complete English record with you to demonstrate that I should have been given an 85.

PARAGRAPH 5: *Writer concludes with a persuasive appeal to review record*

Basic Components

This persuasive composition contains the following structure:

Paragraph 1: An introductory statement of the position the writer takes with regard to a higher grade.
Paragraph 2: The least important reason.
Paragraph 3: The second reason.
Paragraph 4: *The most important reason (ascending order).*
Paragraph 5: A summary statement of the position and a request for change.

Evaluation

This persuasive composition is convincing because it

1. States a definite position and supports it with solid reasons.
2. Arranges those reasons in a logical manner, in *ascending order* (first reason, second reason, then the third and most important reason).
3. Utilizes a variety of sentence forms.
4. Is paragraphed well—introductory position, three reasons, concluding restatement of position.
5. Has paragraph transitions such as "to begin with," "also," "finally and most important," "in short."

FOLLOW-UP EXERCISE

Disagreements with teachers over ratings are common. As a student, you have probably felt that a certain character rating was unfair. Think of such a rating and write a persuasive composition to the teacher in which you give three acceptable reasons, in *ascending order*, why that grade should be changed.

Your pattern should be as follows:

Paragraph 1: Introductory position.
Paragraph 2: Least important reason.
Paragraph 3: Second important reason.
Paragraph 4: *Most important reason.*
Paragraph 5: Restatement of opening position.

Final Analysis

Teachers sometimes make mistakes when grading so many students. Therefore, if you are convinced there was an error, persuade your teacher to change the grade by presenting readily acceptable, well-thought-out reasons. Support these reasons with as many details as you can.

Lesson 3

PERSUADING READERS OF THE SCHOOL PAPER ABOUT THE BEST USE FOR SCHOOL MONEY

THE WRITING TASK

Your student council has raised $2,000 for improving some aspect of the school. While there are differences of opinion as to how the money should be spent, you feel that a good purpose would be served if it were placed into a scholarship fund. Write a composition of about 150 words persuading readers of the school paper that your idea is a sound one.

Writing the Persuasive Composition

ANALYSIS OF THE TASK

What Are You Being Asked to Do?

Persuade your school population that the $2,000 in question be placed in a scholarship fund.

How to Respond

Determine three good reasons with which to support your claim that a scholarship would serve the school best. Arrange these reasons in *ascending order* (first reason, second important reason, then the most important reason). Your outline might look like this:

Reason 1: Treasury money has always been used for trips.
Reason 2: This would be an opportunity to do something useful for the school.
Reason 3: There are a number of needy students who could use assistance for college.

By using the *ascending order*, you have saved your most important reason for last, providing emphasis at the end. The outline is only a structure; now you must develop each reason fully, starting with an impressive statement of your position and ending with a strong restatement of that position.

THE MODEL

Reasons for a Scholarship Fund

The sum of $2,000 raised at our well-attended sports events allows us to do something substantial and lasting for our school. The creation of a scholarship fund to help certain students get into college is, in my opinion, an excellent way to spend that money.

PARAGRAPH 1: *Establishes the need to use money to assist students*

Writing the Persuasive Composition

Prepositional phrase

Complex sentence

Compound sentence

Transition

In the past, as you already know, treasury money has been used to defray the expenses of school trips. While this is an important use of school funds, providing fun and recreation, the time has come to rethink our priorities. Helping needy students get into the colleges of their choice seems like a perfect reason for having a scholarship fund.

Our organization has never really thought of preserving its name in this manner. Other school activities are certainly fine and reason enough for spending treasury money, but the establishment of a scholarship fund will not only make individual students happy but also build motivation for our organization.

The most important reason for the creation of a scholarship fund is that we have a number of bright, achieving students who cannot afford to go to college because of their family circumstances. Therefore, by setting aside the $2,000 to help them gain a higher education, we will be making a contribution worthy of our school organization.

I hope more of you will support my concerted drive for a school scholarship fund for our classmates.

PARAGRAPH 2: *Helping needy students get into college is one important reason*

PARAGRAPH 3: *Starting a scholarship fund to build motivation is another reason*

PARAGRAPH 4: *Aiding bright but poor students is underscored as the most important reason (ascending order)*

PARAGRAPH 5: *An appeal for support serves as the conclusion*

Basic Components

This persuasive composition contains the following structure:

Paragraph 1: The writer's position that a scholarship fund is an ideal way to spend treasury money.

Paragraph 2: The least important reason.

157

Paragraph 3: The second important reason.
Paragraph 4: *The most important reason (ascending order).*
Paragraph 5: The writer's summary statement for support of a scholarship fund.

Evaluation

This persuasive composition is successful because it

1. Is clear as to its purpose.
2. Develops that purpose with three significant reasons.
3. Arranges those three reasons in a convincing manner, in *ascending order* (first important reason, second important reason, then the third and most important reason).
4. Is paragraphed well—strong opening position, three supporting reasons, reemphasis of position.
5. Is coherent in that it sticks to the subject and persuades an audience.

FOLLOW-UP EXERCISE

For every issue, there are many opinions. The job of writing a persuasive composition is to present your position in such a convincing way that those who think differently will reconsider and perhaps support you.

Now, write a similar composition suggesting how a sum of $5,000 raised by selling raffles could be effectively spent in your neighborhood to benefit young people. Develop your position and reasons as follows:

Paragraph 1: State your position clearly and directly.
Paragraph 2: Give your least important reason.
Paragraph 3: Give your second important reason.
Paragraph 4: State your *most important reason*.
Paragraph 5: Restate your opening position.

Final Analysis

Always structure your reasons in outline form first. Select the most important reason and reserve it for last, thus leading your reader to the final "punch." The advantage of using the *ascending order* is that the reader will be more persuaded as he reads on.

Lesson 4

PERSUADING A LOCAL PUBLIC OFFICIAL THAT MORE JOB OPENINGS ARE NEEDED

THE WRITING TASK

In your social studies class, you have been studying the problem of unemployment. Your teacher has asked the class, as an assignment, to write to a public official requesting that more job opportunities be made available. Write a composition of about 150 words to your local public official demanding action on this matter.

ANALYSIS OF THE TASK

What Are You Being Asked to Do?

Convince a local public official that more jobs for the unemployed are essential.

Writing the Persuasive Composition

How to Respond

Think of your position on this issue and state it. Then think of three reasons to support it. Finally, consider how you would like to conclude your paper. The basic pattern might look like this:

Position: Unemployment is a serious problem that can be alleviated by creating jobs for youth.
Reason 1: The young must learn skills early.
Reason 2: Many young people are idle and get into trouble.
Reason 3: People without jobs are a burden for society.
Conclusion: We must act now, before the problem worsens and becomes unsolvable.

With this outline, you already have the structure of your composition. All you have to do now is thread it together with paragraphs, transitional words, clear, interesting sentences, and fuller explanations. Note that reason 3 becomes the most important reason, as is necessary when you are using an *ascending order*.

THE MODEL

Why More Jobs Must Be Created

Unemployment is a serious problem that can be alleviated by creating jobs for youth. Since a vast number of the jobless are teenagers, attention should be paid to this age group. Failure to do so will only perpetuate the problem.

The young must learn skills early if they are to take their place in the world as responsible citizens. Training them before they enter the job market is a wise way to prepare them for the demands of many careers. Since it takes many years to acquire proficiency in many trades, letting them leave school without skills would be a disaster to them as well as to society.

Complex sentence

Simple sentence

PARAGRAPH 1: *Position that youth unemployment is a serious problem*

PARAGRAPH 2: *Skills training for the young is one reason*

160

Writing the Persuasive Composition

Second, because they cannot secure jobs, many of our youth are idle and, as a result, get into trouble. Crime among teenagers is high, largely because they are not involved in anything that would prepare them for life. One sure way to lessen this idleness is to keep them busy learning significant skills that will enable them to get decent jobs when they are ready to seek employment.

Transition — The most important point to consider in arguing for more jobs is that people without them are a burden to society. The costs of supporting them with unemployment insurance are staggering. At a time when our government is faced with so many heavy responsibilities in other areas, such costs can be amply reduced with a program that not only creates jobs but also prepares our youth for their requirements.

Use of semicolon to show close relationship — In conclusion, the recognition that unemployment among teenagers is serious and affects everyone is not quite enough; our government must make a priority of allocating more money for job training and effective performance.

PARAGRAPH 3: *A second reason is that keeping youth engaged in learning skills for jobs will lessen idleness and, therefore, crime*

PARAGRAPH 4: *Societal costs and burdens are stressed as the most important reason (ascending order)*

PARAGRAPH 5: *Spending more money to create job training serves as the conclusion*

Basic Components

This persuasive composition contains the following model structure:

Paragraph 1: The writer's position that unemployment among the young is a problem that must be dealt with.
Paragraph 2: The least important reason.
Paragraph 3: The second important reason.
Paragraph 4: *The most important reason (ascending order).*
Paragraph 5: The writer's summary statement on how unemployment among the young can be resolved.

Evaluation

This persuasive composition is excellent because it

1. Addresses the problem and offers a remedy.
2. Presents three main reasons and explains them fully.
3. Arranges the three reasons convincingly, in *ascending order* (first important reason, second important reason, then third and most important reason).
4. Is paragraphed clearly—opening assessment of the problem, three supporting reasons in favor of more jobs, a conclusion that underscores the urgency of the problem.
5. Utilizes such transitionals as "second," "the most important point," "in conclusion."

FOLLOW-UP EXERCISE

There is never one simple solution to any major problem such as unemployment. While yours may seem the best to you, other people's solutions may also work. Therefore, when you write a persuasive composition, keep in mind that you are convincing readers to change their thinking to yours. Convince and persuade them with as many facts as you can.

Now think of another serious problem facing young people. Write a persuasive composition to your local public official in which you explore the problem and its effects on society. Offer three reasons, in *ascending order*, why your solution is a suitable one.

Final Analysis

Problems have to be analyzed before they can be written about. You can't argue convincingly without building a case for your position. Therefore, establish your thoughts in outline form, regroup your reasons so that the most important one appears at the end, and then make sure your conclusion balances with your opening argument.

Lesson 5

PERSUADING THE TOWN COUNCIL TO IMPROVE A NEEDED SERVICE

THE WRITING TASK

Your town has cut down on garbage pickups because of budget cutbacks. As a result, garbage services have been curtailed, causing a pileup of cans and bags in the streets. Write a composition of about 150 words in which you present convincing reasons why garbage services should be increased rather than decreased.

ANALYSIS OF THE TASK

What Are You Being Asked to Do?

Write 150 words supporting your position that garbage services should be increased rather than decreased.

Writing the Persuasive Composition

How to Respond

First clarify your position by thinking through *why* garbage services are so important. Support the *why* with three convincing reasons. Outline first, as follows:

Paragraph 1: **Position**—Garbage lying about is a health hazard for the community.

Paragraph 2: **Most important reason**—Flies and bugs attack the garbage and become disease carriers.

Paragraph 3: **Second important reason**—Garbage begins to smell bad.

Paragraph 4: **Third important reason**—Cans and bags strewn about the streets are unsightly.

Paragraph 5: **Conclusion**—The town council must act at once before the situation develops into a health problem.

THE MODEL

Increasing Garbage Pickup Services

    The town council's decision to cut back on garbage pickup services because of budgetary problems is unwise. As a result of this decision, more and more garbage in our community is lying about and becoming a health hazard. It is imperative that we increase the pickup services immediately.

    The most important reason is that flies and bugs attack the garbage and become disease carriers. Children who play in the streets will be directly exposed to these carriers. Just think of how terrible it would be if only one child were to come down with dysentery.

PARAGRAPH 1: Writer's position—the need to increase services

PARAGRAPH 2: The most important reason—health hazard (descending order)

Fleshing out reasons

164

Writing the Persuasive Composition

Fleshing out reasons

Another reason for quick removal of garbage is that, as the refuse stands unattended, an offensive smell permeates the neighborhood. This smell is becoming annoying to residents, who are reporting it daily. Many are fearful of possible pollution.

PARAGRAPH 3: *Second reason—possible pollution*

Finally, the endless cans and bags cluttering sidewalks and streets in our attractive neighborhood are very unsightly. It is an ugly situation, to say the least, in a community that can afford the very best for its residents.

PARAGRAPH 4: *Third reason—unsightly appearance*

The reduced services may make sense moneywise, but if the reduction continues, the resulting health problem will cost us more. The town council, in the interests of the community, must act at once to establish a regular garbage service.

PARAGRAPH 5: *Conclusion—the need to act at once to avoid a health problem*

Basic Components

This persuasive composition makes a good case for increased services because it has the following structure:

Paragraph 1: *The writer's position*—based on the town council's decision to cut services.
Paragraph 2: *The most important reason*—a health hazard.
Paragraph 3: *A second reason*—possible pollution.
Paragraph 4: *A third reason*—unsightly appearance.
Paragraph 5: *A conclusion*—that demands immediate action on the part of the town council.

Evaluation

This persuasive composition on increasing garbage pickup services is praiseworthy because it

1. Starts with a clear position and supports it with three convincing reasons.

165

2. Arranges these reasons in a logical manner, in *descending order* (the most important reason, a second important reason, a third important reason).
3. Shows a variety of sentence structure. For example: "The reduced services may make sense moneywise, but if the reduction continues, the resulting health problem will cost us more."
4. Is paragraphed in a unified way.
5. Develops the outline into a full discussion. For example: "This smell is becoming annoying to residents, who are reporting it daily. Many are fearful of possible pollution."

FOLLOW-UP EXERCISE

Think of some problem in your community that can be alleviated. Identify it clearly. Think of convincing evidence to back up your diagnosis of the problem and then offer a possible solution. Write out your argument in no more than 150 words.

Final Analysis

Whatever the problem you are identifying, your task is to establish a strong position, support it convincingly, and conclude with suggestions for a remedy. The scheme of your composition should look like this:

Paragraph 1: Your position stated clearly and strongly.
Paragraph 2: *The most important piece of evidence* to highlight the problem.
Paragraph 3: A second important piece of evidence to highlight the problem.
Paragraph 4: A third important piece of evidence to highlight the problem.
Paragraph 5: A concluding emphasis that something must be done soon.

NOTE: The arrangement of the evidence in *descending order* establishes the seriousness of the problem right away.

Lesson 6

PERSUADING THE SCHOOL PRINCIPAL OF THE NEED FOR A SMOKING ROOM

THE WRITING TASK

Your school forbids smoking, yet there are many students who smoke. There has been discussion of a proposed smoking room, where students could smoke instead of leaving the building. Write a composition of about 150 words in which you present convincing reasons why your principal should accept such a plan.

ANALYSIS OF THE TASK

What Are You Being Asked to Do?

Write 150 words arguing in favor of a smoking room in your school.

Writing the Persuasive Composition

How to Respond

Establish your position that the smoking room is a sound idea. Then support it with three validating reasons. Outline your reasons in *descending order*, as follows:

Paragraph 1: **Position**—A smoking lounge in the school would eliminate certain problems.
Paragraph 2: **Most important reason**—Students sometimes leave school to smoke in the street or in the park.
Paragraph 3: **Second important reason**—The school day is too long for a smoker.
Paragraph 4: **Third important reason**—Students who smoke do not concentrate on their work when they want a cigarette.
Paragraph 5: **Conclusion**—A smoking lounge would not only eliminate some problems but would also create a more comfortable atmosphere.

THE MODEL

The Need for a School Smoking Room

A smoking lounge in our school would eliminate certain problems that seem to persist. In an age of increasing demands for more student rights and self-determination, granting the right to smoke in a limited space is an appropriate measure.

Transitional words

The most important reason for a smoking lounge is that many students leave the school to smoke in the streets or in the park. Their need to light up, apparently, is greater than their need to conform to restrictions. A smoking lounge, therefore, would keep students within the school.

Parenthetical words

PARAGRAPH 1: *Position in favor of a smoking lounge*

PARAGRAPH 2: *The most important reason—students leave the school to smoke (descending order)*

Writing the Persuasive Composition

Transitional words

Further, for any veteran smoker, the school day is too long. Going for six hours without even one cigarette is a difficult task, and those who are subjected to this limitation often react by misbehaving. A smoking lounge would make the smokers among our students more agreeable and cooperative.

Parenthetical words

Third, students who have acquired a smoking habit cannot concentrate on their work when they are itchy for a few puffs. Laying off cigarettes for too long makes them feel restless and distracted. A smoking lounge, obviously, would give them relief and create a better climate for learning.

In conclusion, a smoking lounge will not only eliminate school problems but also create a more comfortable atmosphere.

PARAGRAPH 3: *A second important reason—a schoolday is too long for a smoker*

PARAGRAPH 4: *A third important reason—students cannot concentrate on work when they need a cigarette*

PARAGRAPH 5: *A smoking lounge resolves two needs*

Basic Components

This persuasive composition on the establishment of a school smoking lounge is convincing because it encompasses the following:

Paragraph 1: *The writer's position*—that a school smoking lounge will eliminate problems.

Paragraph 2: *The most important reason*—that the lounge will help to keep students within the school.

Paragraph 3: *A second important reason*—that a lounge will make smokers more agreeable and cooperative.

Paragraph 4: *A third important reason*—that a lounge will create a better climate for learning.

Paragraph 5: *The conclusion*—that a smoking lounge will resolve two critical needs.

Evaluation

This persuasive composition on the establishment of a smoking lounge is superior because it

1. Sets forth the writer's position and thus provides a direction for the essay.
2. Supports that position with three reasons, stated in *descending order* (the most important one, a second one, and a third one).
3. Uses parenthetical words, such as "apparently," "obviously," and "therefore" to emphasize good results.
4. Uses transitional words, such as "the most important reason," "further," "third," and "in conclusion" to bridge paragraphs.
5. Unites five paragraphs smoothly.
6. Structures sentences soundly.
7. Fleshes out reasons to show how this change would improve things.
8. Concludes with a restatement of the opening position.

FOLLOW-UP EXERCISE

Think of a problem in your school that requires a solution. First, determine what your position is. Then list three supporting reasons for your position. Arrange these reasons in *descending order*. Your outline should resemble this:

Paragraph 1: Your position.
Paragraph 2: *The most important reason.*
Paragraph 3: A second important reason.
Paragraph 4: A third important reason.
Paragraph 5: A concluding statement as to the overall results of your proposal.

Final Analysis

A persuasive composition has as its main purpose convincing a person or an audience. Therefore, be sure to develop reasons that will help to change the thinking of the person reading your essay. Your arguments should be concrete, appropriate, and reasonable.

Lesson 7

PERSUADING READERS OF THE SCHOOL PAPER TO PETITION

THE WRITING TASK

Because of rising costs, a decision to do away with the school football team has been made. But since football is very popular among the students, you wish to preserve the team. Write a composition of about 150 words in which you present convincing reasons why the school football team should not be eliminated.

ANALYSIS OF THE TASK

What Are You Being Asked to Do?

Write 150 words supporting your position that the school football team should be retained.

How to Respond

Think through your position carefully, then support it with three convincing, appropriate, reasonable reasons.

Outline first, as follows:

Paragraph 1: **Position**—Football, more than any other sport, unites a school and promotes school spirit. Therefore, our school football team should be supported, not eliminated.

Paragraph 2: **Most important reason**—Our football games are very popular and well attended.

Paragraph 3: **Second important reason**—The football team has had a winning record, a string of victories.

Paragraph 4: **Third important reason**—Football is a necessary outlet for aggressive energy.

Paragraph 5: **Conclusion**—Elimination of the school football team will lessen school spirit, reduce interest in sports, remove a source of pride. Another means of raising funds to perpetuate the team should be found.

THE MODEL

Why Our Football Team Deserves Support

The decision of the school board to eliminate our high-school football team is alarming. Since football, *more than any other sport,* unites a school and promotes spirit, a school football team should be supported, not eliminated.

First of all, football games are very popular and well-attended. Students turn out in great numbers at each game to support our team. The elimination of the team, *therefore,* will erase the kind of morale we have witnessed in the past.

Parenthetical words

Transitional words

PARAGRAPH 1: *The writer's position—football team, because it unites, should be supported*

PARAGRAPH 2: *Most important reason—football games are very popular and well-attended*

Writing the Persuasive Composition

Parenthetical words

Secondly, considering that our football team has had a winning record, why throw it out? If anything, our team has generated pride in the school as a whole. Eliminating the team, now, would cause sadness and depression among our students.

PARAGRAPH 3: *Second important reason—the team has had a successful record*

Transitional words

Thirdly, football is a necessary outlet for aggressive energy. For instance, many top players who would normally be out of school, have a real purpose in attending school. At the same time, they apply themselves to their studies more diligently. Eliminating the team, sadly, would also eliminate these members of the team.

PARAGRAPH 4: *Third important reason—football is a necessary outlet for aggressive energy*

In summation, elimination of the school football team will lessen school spirit, reduce interest in sports, and remove a source of pride. For these reasons, the team should remain active and new means of raising funds for its support should be found.

PARAGRAPH 5: *Conclusion—a new means of support should be found*

Basic Components

This persuasive composition on preserving the school football team presents a solid case because it contains the following:

Paragraph 1: *The writer's position*—on preserving the school football team.
Paragraph 2: *The most important reason.*
Paragraph 3: *A second important reason.*
Paragraph 4: *A third important reason.*
Paragraph 5: *A summation*—that calls for a new means of raising funds with which to support the football team.

Evaluation

This persuasive composition on preserving the school football team is notable because it

1. Presents a justifiable position.

Writing the Persuasive Composition

2. Arranges three reasons in a logical manner and in *descending order* (the most important reason, a second important reason, a third important reason).
3. Shows complexity of sentence structure: "Since football, more than any other sport, unites a school and promotes spirit, a school football team should be supported, not eliminated."
4. Is paragraphed coherently.
5. Shows the effect of eliminating the team: "Eliminating the team, now, would cause sadness and depression among our students."
6. Uses transitional words—such as "First of all," "secondly," "thirdly," and "for instance"—to connect paragraph units.
7. Employs parenthetical words, such as "more than any other sport," "therefore," and "now" to emphasize the potential loss.
8. Is free of major mechanical and grammatical errors.

FOLLOW-UP EXERCISE

A decision to eliminate physical education from the school program has been made. Write a persuasive composition of about 150 words in which you support a clear position with three convincing reasons. Be sure to arrange these reasons in *descending order*.

Final Analysis

Always ask yourself this question: "Why am I taking this stand?" The answer should lead to a consistent pattern of thinking that makes the initial argument seem forceful and important. The *descending order* pattern highlights the most important point first, allowing you to zero in on the problem immediately. Thus, the plan of your writing should be:

Paragraph 1: Your position stated clearly and directly.
Paragraph 2: *The most important reason* for your position.
Paragraph 3: A second important reason for your position.
Paragraph 4: A third important reason for your position.
Paragraph 5: A summation in which you restate the initial position and call for a more effective measure.

Lesson 8

PERSUADING A TV STATION TO UPGRADE QUALITY

WRITING TASK

For the most part, you observe, television programming is dull, insulting and unengaging. It is your opinion that television viewing is largely a waste of time. Write a composition of about 150 words in which you try to convince a TV station to upgrade the quality of its programming.

ANALYSIS OF THE TASK

What Are You Being Asked to Do?

Write 150 words supporting your position that the quality of television programming should be upgraded.

How to Respond

Make your position statement clear and direct. Then offer supporting evidence that shows a *cause-and-effect relationship*. You may

Writing the Persuasive Composition

structure your composition this way:

Paragraph 1: **Position**—Commercial television, for the most part, is dull, insulting, and unengaging. The quality of the shows presented on a regular basis leaves much to be desired.

Paragraph 2: **Cause**—Soap operas try to capture dilemmas and life situations.
Effect—Instead, they create a dull picture of people's struggles to cope with the world.

Paragraph 3: **Cause**—Family-situation programs present the daily struggles of ordinary people in a supposedly realistic manner.
Effect—The programs convey a distorted view of the human condition and give people false hope.

Paragraph 4: **Cause**—Crime programs, because of their unremitting emphasis on violence, soon become stale and uninteresting.
Effect—Viewers become jaded about crime and indifferent to human suffering.

Paragraph 5: **Conclusion**—Television is a medium that can foster learning and awareness. Instead of insulting the viewing audience, it should lift the spirit and offer an optimistic view of human possibility.

THE MODEL

Upgrading the Quality of TV Programming

Commercial television, for the most part, is dull, insulting and unengaging. The quality of the shows presented regularly leaves much to be desired. What is needed is quality programming that entertains as well as instructs.

PARAGRAPH 1: *The writer's argument that television programming needs change*

[Cause 1]
[Result 1]
Soap operas, such as "A Quest for Life" try to capture human dilemmas and life situations. Instead, they convey a trite picture of people's struggles to cope with the world. The audience cries but never gains genuine insights.

PARAGRAPH 2: *Soap operas convey a trite picture of human problems*

176

Writing the Persuasive Composition

Cause 2	Family-situation programs, such as "Little House on the Prairie," present the daily struggles of ordinary people in a supposedly realistic way.	PARAGRAPH 3: *Family-situation programs also convey distorted views*
Result 2	Actually, these programs convey a distorted and overly-simplified view of the human condition, and, therefore, give people false hope. Viewers come away with false notions that cannot help them resolve their own struggles.	
Cause 3	Crime programs, because of their emphasis on violence, become boring and dull the senses. The constant exposure to inhuman acts tends to make viewers take crime for granted rather than condemn it.	PARAGRAPH 4: *Crime programs cause acceptance and indifference*
Result 3	The result is that they become jaded and indifferent to human suffering.	
	Television is a medium that could promote learning and awareness. Instead of insulting the viewing audience, it should lift their spirits and offer an optimistic view of human possibilities. Only with better-quality programming can this come about.	PARAGRAPH 5: *Conclusion about the potential of television*

Basic Components

This persuasive composition on upgrading television programming is organized as follows:

Paragraph 1: *The writer's argument*—that much of television needs change.
Paragraph 2: *Cause and effect*—how soap operas give a trite picture of peoples's struggles.
Paragraph 3: *Cause and effect*—how family-situation programs convey a distorted view of the human condition.
Paragraph 4: *Cause and effect*—how crime programs encourage indifference to human suffering.
Paragraph 5: *A conclusion*—that television can do much more to teach people and make them more aware.

Evaluation

This persuasive composition on upgrading the quality of television programming is excellent because it

1. Takes a clear position and validates it with three convincing reasons.
2. Arranges these reasons in a logical manner, by *cause and effect*.
3. Has a variety of sentence structure. "Family-situation programs, such as 'Little House on the Prairie,' present the daily struggles of ordinary people in a supposedly realistic way."
4. Divides ideas into smooth paragraphs.
5. Shows how current programming influences feelings and attitudes.
6. Is free of major mechanical and grammatical errors.

FOLLOW-UP EXERCISE

Determine what you consider to be a deficiency in movies today. State that deficiency as a position. Support it with three convincing reasons, arranged according to *cause and effect*. Then write a persuasive composition of about 150 words in which you suggest a significant improvement. Structure your paper as follows:

Paragraph 1: Your position on movies of today.
Paragraph 2: Cause 1 and effect 1.
Paragraph 3: Cause 2 and effect 2.
Paragraph 4: Cause 3 and effect 3.
Paragraph 5: Concluding statement on movies of today.

Final Analysis

Evaluating the quality of modern movies is best done by giving specific examples of films and stating how they influence viewers' thinking and behavior. Therefore, whatever you say concerning a type of film, always offer specific examples.

Organization in terms of *cause-and-effect* relationships is the best way to show influence and outcome. This is an excellent technique to use when a medium as important as film is being evaluated.

Lesson 9

PERSUADING THE LOCAL POLICE TO PATROL MORE OFTEN

THE WRITING TASK

Your neighborhood has been the scene of a series of crimes that the residents have found very disturbing. Therefore, many of the local people have called for more and better police protection. Write a composition of about 150 words in which you present convincing reasons why the police should patrol more frequently.

ANALYSIS OF THE TASK

What Are You Being Asked to Do?

Write 150 words supporting your position that the police should patrol more frequently in your neighborhood.

Writing the Persuasive Composition

How to Respond

Clearly define your position that patrols are needed. Then support that statement with three appropriate, relevant reasons. Outline as follows:

Paragraph 1: **Position**—Recent acts of crime in our neighborhood have clearly been disturbing to the residents. More frequent police patrols will, at least, deter criminal acts in the future.

Paragraph 2: **Cause**—Many homes have been broken into.
Effect—Homeowners are fearful of leaving their homes for any length of time.

Paragraph 3: **Cause**—Parked cars have been damaged, with their windows broken and tires punctured.
Effect—Residents have to garage cars for fear of vandalism.

Paragraph 4: **Cause**—Shrubs, trees, and plants have been torn apart and strewn over lawns.
Effect—Residents are compelled to form patrols to protect property.

Paragraph 5: **Conclusion**—The many criminal acts in our neighborhood have created tension and concern. More frequent police patrols are not merely requested; they are demanded.

THE MODEL

The Need for More Frequent Police Patrols

Recent acts of crime in our neighborhood are clearly disturbing the residents. More frequent police patrols will, at the least, deter criminal acts in the future.

PARAGRAPH 1: *Writer's position on the need for more police patrols*

Since many homes have been broken into and vandalized, homeowners are fearful of leaving their homes for any length of time. Police patrols would help to discourage would-be burglars.

Complex sentences to show cause-effect relationships

PARAGRAPH 2: *Vandalism and its effect on residents*

180

Writing the Persuasive Composition

Complex sentences to show cause-effect relationships

Because so many parked cars have been damaged, windows broken, and tires punctured, residents have had to garage their cars for fear of vandalism. More police patrols would certainly help to minimize such incidents.

PARAGRAPH 3: *Damaged cars and their effect on the residents*

Because shrubs, trees, and plants have been torn apart and strewn over lawns, residents have felt compelled to form their own patrols to protect property. Why should these people have to become guardians of property when this is the job of the police?

PARAGRAPH 4: *Destruction of lawns and its effect on the residents*

The many criminal acts in our neighborhood have created tension and concern. More frequent police patrols are not merely requested; they are demanded.

PARAGRAPH 5: *Conclusion that police patrols are demanded*

Basic Components

This persuasive composition on getting increased neighborhood police patrols is structured as follows:

Paragraph 1: States the *writer's position* on the need for more police patrols.
Paragraph 2: Shows how vandalism (*cause*) creates fear (*effect*).
Paragraph 3: Describes how damaged cars (*cause*) creates a compulsion to garage cars (*effect*).
Paragraph 4: Explains that destruction of lawns (*cause*) has created a need to form patrols (*effect*).
Paragraph 5: States the *conclusion* that the tension and worry (*cause*) generated by criminal acts demand more police patrols (*effect*).

Evaluation

This persuasive composition on getting increased neighborhood police patrols is exemplary because it

1. States a sound position and supports it with evidence.

Writing the Persuasive Composition

2. Arranges this evidence in a *cause-and-effect* pattern.
3. Uses complex sentences to show the *cause-and-effect* relationship, for example, "Because so many parked cars have been damaged, windows broken, and tires punctured, residents have had to garage their cars for fear of vandalism."
4. Shows how police patrols would help: "More police patrols would certainly help to minimize such incidents."
5. Devotes a separate paragraph to each *cause-and-effect* piece of evidence.
6. Reaffirms the opening statement in the concluding paragraph.
7. Is free of major mechanical and grammatical errors.

FOLLOW-UP EXERCISE

Pinpoint a problem in your own neighborhood that might be alleviated with more help from the police. State the problem, outline your position with regard to the role of the police, and offer three convincing pieces of evidence that show a *cause-and-effect* relationship. Write your argument out as a persuasive composition of about 150 words. Structure your paper as follows:

Paragraph 1: Your position on the need for more help from the police.
Paragraph 2: Cause 1 and effect 1.
Paragraph 3: Cause 2 and effect 2.
Paragraph 4: Cause 3 and effect 3.
Paragraph 5: Your conclusion, reaffirming the opening position statement.

Final Analysis

Organization in terms of a *cause-and-effect* pattern is an ideal way of dealing with a neighborhood problem, because it allows you to show how a particular condition (cause) results in a certain attitude (result). Be sure, in structuring your sentences, to use the complex type of sentence, for example: "Because of recent traffic deaths in our neighborhood, parents are refusing to allow their children to play outside." The above example shows:

The Cause: "Because of recent traffic deaths in our neighborhood," and
The Result: "parents are refusing to allow their children to play outside."

Lesson 10

PERSUADING THE LOCAL SCHOOL BOARD TO COMPLETE A PROJECT

THE WRITING TASK

The construction of a swimming pool in the high school was recently begun. But, because of a lack of funds, a decision to stop construction was made by the local board of education. Write a persuasive composition of about 150 words in which you establish a basis for completion of the swimming pool.

ANALYSIS OF THE TASK

What Are You Being Asked to Do?

Write 150 words establishing your argument that the high-school swimming pool be completed.

How to Respond

Write your position statement supporting the need for a swimming pool. Then support that position statement with three significant reasons. Structure your paper in this way:

Paragraph 1: **Position**—The swimming pool, proposed by the board of education and actually begun, is a necessity. For many reasons, it is a promise that should be kept.

Paragraph 2: **Reason 1**—Exactly one year ago, a referendum was signed supporting the project.

Paragraph 3: **Reason 2**—Six months ago, plans for the swimming pool were made as part of an expanded physical education program.

Paragraph 4: **Reason 3**—A swimming team was organized, and competition with teams of other schools was planned.

Paragraph 5: **Conclusion**—The refusal of our board of education to advance funds to complete the high-school swimming pool is a downright insult to the community, which had looked forward to such great possibilities.

THE MODEL

The Need for a High School Swimming Pool

The high-school swimming pool, proposed by the board of education and actually begun, is a necessity. For many reasons, it is a promise that should be kept.

Exactly one year ago, a referendum was signed supporting the project. The majority of taxpayers indicated that they wanted it, since the advantages to the community had become apparent.

Six months ago, plans for the swimming pool were made as part of an expanded physical education program. Classes were to include swimming lessons, teams were to be organized, and competition was to begin.

Chronological arrangement of reasons supporting the completion of the high school swimming pool.

PARAGRAPH 1: *Writer's position that a swimming pool is a necessity*

PARAGRAPH 2: *Reason 1— taxpayers wanted it*

PARAGRAPH 3: *Reason 2— Plans were already under way*

184

Writing the Persuasive Composition

> *Chronological arrangement of reasons supporting the completion of the high school swimming pool*

In fact, just three months ago, students were selected for a team on the basis of tryouts. They had been meeting afternoons, practicing strokes for grueling hours. The entire school was excited about the prospect of having, perhaps, a winning team.

The refusal of our board of education to advance funds to complete the high-school swimming pool is a downright insult to a community that has anticipated such great possibilities. To avert a negative community reaction, a means to complete the construction should be found.

PARAGRAPH 4: *Reason 3—A team was selected for competition*

PARAGRAPH 5: *Conclusion that a means to complete the pool should be found*

Basic Components

This persuasive composition on the completion of a high-school swimming pool contains the following:

Paragraph 1: *Position*—The writer's position that a promise made is a promise kept.

Paragraph 2: *Reason 1*—that the taxpayers voted for the pool by means of a referendum.

Paragraph 3: *Reason 2*—that school scheduling of swim classes had already begun.

Paragraph 4: *Reason 3*—that a school swimming team had already been selected and had generated enthusiasm.

Paragraph 5: *Conclusion*—that some means to complete the construction must be found.

Evaluation

This persuasive composition is excellent because it

1. States the writer's position and supports it with convincing reasons.
2. Arranges those reasons in *chronological order*.
   Paragraph 2: "Exactly one year ago . . ."
   Paragraph 3: "Six months ago . . ."
   Paragraph 4: "Just three months ago . . ."

185

Writing the Persuasive Composition

3. Includes sophisticated sentences, such as: "Six months ago, plans for the swimming pool were made as part of an expanded physical education program."
4. Develops each reason fully in separate paragraphs.
5. Is consistent throughout in its urgent argument to save the swimming pool.
6. Concludes with a sincere but strong demand that some way be found to complete the pool.
7. Is free of major grammatical and mechanical errors.

FOLLOW-UP EXERCISE

Your local board of education originally approved a plan to construct a needed gymnasium but, because of limited funds, has now voted to abandon it. Write a persuasive composition of about 150 words in which you advance your position that a gymnasium is vitally needed. Support that position with three reasons, arranged *chronologically*, and conclude with a suggestion that will resolve the issue. Structure your paper as follows:

Paragraph 1: Your position that the proposed school gymnasium should be completed.
Paragraph 2: Reason 1.
Paragraph 3: Reason 2.
Paragraph 4: Reason 3.
Paragraph 5: Your conclusion urging the board to obtain funds with which to complete the project.

Final Analysis

Placing evidence in support of a position in *chronological order* (the earliest piece of evidence, the next in time, and a third later in time) gives a full picture of a situation that requires examination and solution. Therefore you will do best to arrange all your facts in that order. Then you can decide which three you will use to validate your argument.

Lesson 11

PERSUADING A LEGISLATOR TO SUPPORT INCREASED FUNDS FOR SCHOOLS

THE WRITING TASK

Your state legislature has reduced appropriation for the schools, thus curtailing many services and programs. Write a persuasive composition of about 150 words in which you advance the position that reduced appropriations mean reduced education for the students.

ANALYSIS OF THE TASK

What Are You Being Asked to Do?

Write 150 words designed to convince a state legislator that more money for educational services is needed.

Writing the Persuasive Composition

How to Respond

First write your position statement clearly. Then support that position statement with three reasons arranged in a *contrast pattern*. Structure your paper as follows:

Paragraph 1: **Position**—The recent cut in educational funds by the state legislature spells doom for our schools and the students who attend them. Services and programs so vitally needed for the education of our youth will go by the wayside.

Paragraph 2: **Contrast 1**—Deerborn School District continues to show gains in its intramural sports competition, while our high school will lose both its football and basketball teams because of budget cutbacks. The consequences to morale and sportsmanship will be serious.

Paragraph 3: **Contrast 2**—Similarly, the nearby Selwin schools, with which we have been competing for the last several years, will continue to present school plays, while our school productions will be eliminated. When you think of the hundreds of students keenly involved in theater arts, the absence of drama will be a staggering loss.

Paragraph 4: **Contrast 3**—Also, in view of all the awards our literary publication has won in the last ten years, the loss of so significant a co-curricular activity is saddening. What is a school without some evidence of student literary activity? The answer is obvious.

Paragraph 5: **Conclusion**—Drastic cutbacks in school appropriations, for whatever reasons, are one sure way to destroy what our schools have worked so hard to build. Such curtailments, obviously, will not only eradicate programs and services but transform our schools into cultural deserts.

Writing the Persuasive Composition

THE MODEL

More Money Is Needed in Our Schools

The recent cut in educational funds by the state legislature spells doom for our schools and the students who attend them. Services and programs so vitally needed for the education of our youth will go by the wayside unless this decision is reversed.

Contrasting elements: Deerborn School District, east of us, continues to show gains in its intramural sports competition, while our high school will lose both its football and basketball teams because of budget cutbacks. The consequences to morale and sportsmanship will be serious.

Similarly, Selwin, our neighboring district, with which we have been in competition for the last several years, will continue to present school plays, while our school productions will be eliminated. When you think of the hundreds of students keenly involved in theater arts, the absence of drama will be a staggering loss.

Also, in view of all the awards our literary publication has won in the last ten years, the loss of so significant a co-curricular activity is saddening. What is a school without some evidence of student literary activity? The answer is obvious.

Drastic cutbacks in school appropriations, for whatever reasons, are one sure way to destroy what our schools have worked so hard to build. Such curtailments, obviously, will not only eradicate programs and services

---

PARAGRAPH 1: *The writer's position that school cutbacks mean serious loss of services*

PARAGRAPH 2: *Contrast 1—Deerborn School District will continue its sports while we will see teams eliminated*

PARAGRAPH 3: *Contrast 2—Selwin Schools will shine dramatically while we see the end of school plays*

PARAGRAPH 4: *Contrast 3—We won awards for our literary publication before, but now we will have no publication*

PARAGRAPH 5: *Conclusion—drastic cutbacks will destroy what the schools have built*

```
but transform our schools into cultural
deserts. To avert this, money for the
support of threatened programs must
somehow be found.
```

Basic Components

This persuasive composition breaks down as follows:

Paragraph 1: *Position*—the writer's argument that reduced money for education spells doom for our schools.
Paragraph 2: *Contrast Reason 1*—Deerborn School District will continue to compete in sports, while our high school will lose teams.
Paragraph 3: *Contrast Reason 2*—The Selwin schools will continue to enter dramatic competition, while our school productions will be eliminated.
Paragraph 4: *Contrast Reason 3*—though our literary publication won awards in the past, it will now have to cease publication.
Paragraph 5: *Conclusion*—Drastic cutbacks will destroy programs and services.

Evaluation

This persuasive composition successfully condemns cutbacks in education because it

1. States a strong position and defends it well.
2. Arranges three reasons in *contrasting patterns*.
3. Uses contrasts with previous situations to demonstrate loss of valuable programs.
4. Treats each contrast as a separate paragraph.
5. Is consistent throughout in its defense of threatened programs.
6. Concludes with an urgent message to appropriate needed funds.
7. Uses the conjunction "while" to contrast elements, as in "similarly Selwin, our neighboring district, with which we have been in competition for the last several years, will continue to

Writing the Persuasive Composition

present school plays, *while* our school productions will be eliminated."

FOLLOW-UP EXERCISE

The state legislature has voted to withdraw funds for driver education programs in your schools. Write a persuasive composition of about 150 words in which you argue that the loss of this program will be a great burden to the students. When you decide on your reasons in support of your position, arrange them in a *contrast pattern*. Structure your paper as follows:

Paragraph 1: Your position that funds for a driver education program are needed.
Paragraph 2: Contrast Reason 1.
Paragraph 3: Contrast Reason 2.
Paragraph 4: Contrast Reason 3.
Paragraph 5: Conclusion urging immediate action.

Final Analysis

The *contrast pattern* of arranging reasons in support of a position is effective because it demonstrates how a situation will change from good to bad. Your contrasts may be based on (1) a previous program or service, (2) a neighboring school district, (3) previous honors or awards, (4) former successes, (5) student attitudes.

Lesson 12

PERSUADING PARENTS TO HELP FINANCE A CAR

THE WRITING TASK

You have your heart set on buying a car, but your parents feel that you should wait until you are older. Discussions with them don't seem to alter their view. Write a persuasive composition of about 150 words in which you present a convincing argument that you are indeed ready to assume the responsibility of owning and maintaining a car.

ANALYSIS OF THE TASK
What Are You Being Asked to Do?

Write 150 words convincing your parents that you are responsible enough to buy and maintain a car.

How to Respond

Decide on your position and then think of three supporting reasons. Using the *comparison pattern*, refer to other people and situations to strengthen your argument. Structure your paper as follows:

Writing the Persuasive Composition

Paragraph 1: **Position**—Like friends and other people my age, I am old enough and responsible enough to drive and maintain a car.

Paragraph 2: **Comparison Reason 1**—Most of the people in my class have their own cars, which they keep up themselves.

Paragraph 3: **Comparison Reason 2**—Dean James's parents bought him a car for his birthday, and he has had no trouble looking after it.

Paragraph 4: **Comparison Reason 3**—My best friend, Don Whalen, worked part-time till he had saved enough money to buy a used car. He has now had it for a year.

Paragraph 5: **Conclusion**—It is very common, as you can see, for young people my age to attend school and, at the same time, to own and maintain a car.

THE MODEL

I Can Be Responsible For a Car

Like friends and others my age, I am old enough and responsible enough to drive and maintain a car. Our generation, different from yours, matures faster and assumes responsibilities earlier. Among us, the wish to own a car is not at all unreasonable.

PARAGRAPH 1: *The writer's assertion that he is responsible enough to have a car*

Most of the people in my class have their own cars, which they keep up on their own. They manage to meet their upkeep expenses by working and saving. Instead of wasting their earnings on silly things, they purposefully use them to keep their cars in good condition.

Expanded details

PARAGRAPH 2: *Comparison 1 Most young people today own cars*

Dean James's parents bought him a car for his birthday, and he has had no trouble supporting it. Since he knows a great deal about repairs, he fixes whatever defects crop up and therefore saves a lot of money. Because I too

PARAGRAPH 3: *Comparison 2 Dean James can repair his own car*

Writing the Persuasive Composition

---

know so much about automotive mechanics, I am sure I will be able to make my own repairs.

My best friend, Don Whalen, worked part-time until he had saved enough money to buy a used car. He has now had it for a year. The experience of earning it on his own has made him a better person—more reliable and self-sufficient. I am sure that if I had a car, I too would grow in this way.

It is very common, as you can see, for young people my age to attend school and, at the same time, to own and maintain a car. I see no conflict with regard to doing well in school and having the pleasure of having my own car. Unlike your generation, which was more concerned with survival, ours looks to the means of enjoyment that make life worth living.

Expanded details

PARAGRAPH 4: *Comparison 3 Don Whalen worked to save for a car*

PARAGRAPH 5: *Conclusion— Owning a car represents no real conflict*

Basic Components

This persuasive composition comprises the following:

Paragraph 1: *Position*—The writer's assertion that he is responsible enough to have a car and that the wish to own one is not considered unreasonable among members of his generation.

Paragraph 2: *Comparison 1*—Most members of this generation already own their own cars.

Paragraph 3: *Comparison 2*—Dean James is an example of a young person who can maintain a car because he knows how to repair it.

Paragraph 4: *Comparison 3*—Don Whalen worked to save money to buy a car; as a result, he has become a better person.

Paragraph 5: *Conclusion*—It is common for young people of this generation to have cars, the possession of which represents no real conflict.

Writing the Persuasive Composition

Evaluation

This persuasive composition is exemplary because it

1. States the writer's position and supports it with three convincing reasons.
2. Arranges those reasons in order of *comparison*, making reference to other young people who already have their own cars.
3. Expands basic comparison details into fuller pictures of a situation, as in

   Paragraph 4: "The experience of earning it on his own has made him a better person—more reliable and self-sufficient. I am sure that if I had a car, I too would grow in this way."
4. Incorporates sophisticated sentences, as in

   Paragraph 5: "It is very common, as you can see, for young people my age to attend school and, at the same time, to own and maintain a car."
5. Is consistent, throughout, in its argument that the writer is mature enough to own a car.
6. Concludes with a generalization about youth today and a restatement of the argument that the writer can do what other young people have done.
7. Is free of major grammatical and mechanical errors.

FOLLOW-UP EXERCISE

You are faced with a conflict with your parents. While you insist that you are old enough to travel alone during the summer, your parents maintain that such an experience should be postponed till you are older. Write a persuasive composition of about 150 words in which you justify your position that you can handle the problems of traveling alone during the summer. Arrange your reasons in order of *comparison*, as follows:

Paragraph 1: Your position that the experience of traveling alone during the summer is worthwhile.
Paragraph 2: Comparison Reason 1.
Paragraph 3: Comparison Reason 2.
Paragraph 4: Comparison Reason 3.
Paragraph 5: Your conclusion that such an experience will benefit you in many ways.

Writing the Persuasive Composition

Final Analysis

The *comparison pattern* of arranging reasons to justify an argument helps you to refer to people and situations that support your position.

Therefore, use names, specific events, and exact details to describe these comparative situations. In short, comparisons strengthen your argument.

7

TWO MODEL TESTS

The model tests in this section provide further drill on your three required writing tasks: the business letter of complaint, the report, the persuasive composition.

The best way to use this section effectively is to pretend that you are actually taking the Regents Competency Test in Writing. First, complete Model Test 1. Read the model questions carefully, outline your notes, and write the required number of words. When you have finished the test, read the model essays for both form and content. Compare each of your writing tasks with the corresponding model. Determine whether or not you have: (1) written enough to satisfy the required number of words, (2) fulfilled the question satisfactorily, (3) organized your details in a logical pattern, (4) begun and ended each writing task with a clear opening and concluding statement, and (5) expressed your ideas skillfully. If not, revise your writing samples until you feel you have done a good job. Use the same procedure with Model Test 2.

Remember that doing well on the Regents Competency Test in Writing requires constant practice. Practice means frequent writing with a model guide. The models provided in this section will enable you to judge the quality of your writing.

Model Test 1

REGENTS COMPETENCY TEST—WRITING

Part I—Business Letter

Directions

Use the proper business-letter form in responding to the situation below.

You saw an ad in the newspaper offering a three-speed Rogers bicycle at a sale price of $80.99. When you arrived at the store, you were told by the salesman that only three such bicycles were available at that price and that they were already sold.

Write a business letter concerning the problem to the store at this address: Consumer Cycle Company, 80 Washington Road, Albany, NY 12234.

When you write your letter, remember to:
- *Fulfill the situation above.*
- *Offer a solution.*
- *Follow the format of a proper business letter.*

Part II—Report

Directions

The report you write should be based on the details below. Before you begin to write, arrange these details in proper order.

Your health education class is studying marriage and family living. Your parents' association is meeting to consider a proposal to start a course called "Marriage and Family Living" in your school. Your teacher has asked you to write a report of the meeting for your class. Your notes are in the box below.

Held in the auditorium
Started at 8:30, ended at 11:00
A lot of pros and cons from parents
Coffee and doughnuts served
President directed the meeting
One parent shouted the home should teach this concern
Guest speaker arrived late
Dr. James Smith spoke about the importance of preparing students for life
A planning committee report was read
No real consensus was reached
There are many values to such a course
Many parents are afraid of such a course
The high rate of divorce is a real concern
Students would be allowed to consider their future roles as parents

---

Arrange these notes in proper order. Then write a report that includes all the information in the notes.

Part III—Composition

Directions

Write an essay in which you try to convince your parents that your opinion on the topic described below is sound.

You try to persuade your parents to go along with your desire to take a job after school. Your parents seem to feel you should devote all your time to your studies and not sacrifice it for the sake of earning money.

Write a composition of at least 200 words explaining your position to your parents and why you feel so strongly about it. Give at least two reasons. Explain each reason.

Diagnosis

MODEL PAPERS

Part I—The Business Letter

<table>
<tr><td></td><td>56 Rose Boulevard
Detroit, MI 50540
January 4, 1983</td><td>Heading</td></tr>
<tr><td>Inside
Address</td><td>Manager
Consumer Cycle Company
80 Washington Road
Albany, NY 12234</td><td></td></tr>
<tr><td>Salutation</td><td>Dear Manager:</td><td></td></tr>
</table>

    I wish to register a complaint about your sale policy, which is obviously misleading.

    On December 30, I saw an ad in the newspaper telling about a sale price of $80.99 for a three-speed Rogers bicycle. When I arrived on December 31, the salesman informed me that this sale applied to three bikes only. When I asked to see those three, he added that they were already sold.

PARAGRAPH 1:
The <u>cause</u> of the complaint—misleading ad

PARAGRAPH 2:
Details to support the cause of the complaint

> I was not only frustrated but very distressed that a newspaper ad could be so misleading. Your policy will only succeed in annoying the public and eventually driving customers away. I, for one, certainly will not return.
>
> Regretfully yours,
> Joyce Brooks

PARAGRAPH 3: Effects of policy on writer and others

Complimentary close

Signature

Diagnosis

This business letter of complaint:

1. Satisfies the task.
2. Is clear and direct.
3. Is organized smoothly, as follows:

   Paragraph 1: The purpose for writing.
   Paragraph 2: Background information on the complaint.
   Paragraph 3: A concluding personal feeling and expectation.

4. Is free of major mechanical errors.
5. Arranges details logically, from a *cause* (misleading advertising) to an *effect* (frustration and distress).

Part II—Report

> Our local P.T.A. met on Tuesday, December 19, 1982, to consider a proposal for a course called "Marriage and Family Living." There was a big turnout of parents in the high school auditorium. **After coffee and doughnuts were served, the President called the people to order and began to direct the meeting, starting at 8:30 P.M.** A planning committee report was read before the proceedings got under way.

Complex sentence

PARAGRAPH 1: Notes on beginning of meeting—where, when, who

Two Model Tests

> [Simple sentence] The guest speaker, who arrived late, spoke about the importance of preparing students for life. Dr. James Smith stressed the many values of a course such as "Marriage and Family Living." Parents [Relative clause] who rose to react to the talk aired their views, expressing the feeling that the school would not handle this subject responsibly, concern about the high rate of divorce, and the conviction that students themselves should be allowed to make choices as to their future roles as parents.
>
> [Prepositional phrase] At 11 P.M., the meeting came to a close; no real consensus was reached. As the parents left the auditorium, one father shouted that the home should teach children about marriage and family living.

PARAGRAPH 2: Notes on speaker and main issue of meeting—a new course

Parental concerns

PARAGRAPH 3: Notes on the close of the meeting—a shouting father (chronological order)

Diagnosis

This report on a P.T.A. meeting:

1. Includes all the notes given.
2. Arranges those notes *chronologically*.
3. Structures three paragraphs, as follows:

    Paragraph 1: Where the meeting was held and how it got under way.

    Paragraph 2: The main part of the meeting, when the issue was taken up.

    Paragraph 3: The end of the meeting and a father's last words.

4. Incorporates a variety of sentence structure—simple as well as complex sentences.
5. Contains phrases and clauses that add depth to the report.
6. Is free of major mechanical errors.

Part III—Persuasive Composition

I have reached a point in my life where working after school is necessary for my well-being. *Despite* my parents' protests against my working, I feel that holding a job will help me in many ways.

Though my parents argue that my first duty is to my schoolwork, I believe I can handle both school and a job. Since I get out of school at 2 P.M., I have enough time to work from 3 P.M. to 7 P.M. and still complete all my homework.

Despite their insistence that I rely on them for spending money, I would like to earn my own. Earning money is a sign of maturity. Also, I would like to be self-sufficient, even though my parents want me to depend on them.

While they also urge me to do well in school and have a good time and not burden myself with a job, I believe that working for someone else will not interfere with the fun in my life because I will have time to be with my friends on weekends.

Since both my parents are dead set against my taking a job after school, it is important for me to convince them, for the above reasons, that I am old and mature enough to assume this added responsibility.

(Left margin note: Conjunctions that establish contrast)

PARAGRAPH 1: The writer states his position on work

PARAGRAPH 2: Writer states reason 1, in contrast with parents' view

PARAGRAPH 3: Writer states reason 2, in contrast with parents' view

PARAGRAPH 4: Writer states reason 3, in contrast with parents' view

PARAGRAPH 5: Concludes with a definite purpose

Diagnosis

This persuasive composition on working after school:

1. Is clear about the writer's position.
2. Supports that position with three concrete reasons.
3. Develops those three reasons by *contrast* with the views of the parents.
4. Concludes with a definite purpose.
5. Constructs sentences with key conjunctions to highlight differences between writer and parents.
6. Is free of major mechanical errors.

HOW TO EVALUATE YOUR PROGRESS

After you have studied the section "Diagnosis: Model Papers," you should have a good idea as to what constitutes an acceptable business letter, report, and persuasive composition. The same components used to illustrate good writing in the samples should appear in your own writing.

To judge whether you are indeed making gains, ask yourself these questions after you have completed a particular writing task:

WRITER'S CHECKLIST		
Business Letter	Yes	No
1. Did I explain the problem?		
2. Did I make clear what I want the company to do?		
3. Did I give complete and correct information?		
4. Did I use an acceptable business letter form?		

Two Model Tests

Report	Yes	No
1. Did I carry out the given task?		
2. Did I use all the notes?		
3. Did I organize the notes in a certain pattern?		
4. Have I used paragraphs to show separation of ideas?		
5. Did I review my paper for proper sentence structure, grammatical correctness, and proper usage?		

Composition	Yes	No
1. Did I address myself to the question?		
2. Did I state a clear position?		
3. Did I support that position with sufficient reasons?		
4. Did I arrange these reasons into a certain pattern?		
5. Did I conclude with a sentence that relates to my opening?		
6. Did I write enough words?		
7. Did I review my paper for proper sentence structure, grammatical correctness, and proper usage?		

Now continue with Model Test 2.

Model Test 2

REGENTS COMPETENCY TEST—WRITING

Part I—Business Letter

Directions

Use the proper business-letter form in responding to the situation below.

A local carpeting company keeps calling to offer a special price for carpet cleaning. Though you say no each time, they continue to call.

Write a business letter concerning the problem to the store at this address: Thorough Carpet Cleaning, 15 Rogers Road, Brooklyn, NY 11234.

When you write your letter, remember to:

- Fulfill the situation above.
- Offer a solution.
- Follow the format of a proper business letter.

Part II—Report

Directions

The report you write should be based on the details below. Before you begin to write, arrange these details in proper order.

Your English teacher has asked the class to write a report on an interesting place the students visited during their summer vacation. It so happens you took notes on a visit to Westminster Abbey in London. These notes are in the box below.

> Located in the heart of London
> Enormous stained-glass windows
> Several altars richly decorated
> Several small chapels within the abbey
> Crypts of famous people
> Icons and statuary everywhere
> A small museum of sacred relics
> A very high-domed ceiling
> Entered the abbey July 4
> Revisited on July 9
> Reviewed the tour books first
> Hired a guide to escort us

Arrange these notes in proper order. Then write a report that includes all the information in the notes.

Part III—Composition

Directions

Write an essay in which you try to convince your neighbors that your opinion on the topic described below is sound.

You try to persuade your neighbors to band together to sign a petition to get a "stop" sign up at a dangerous intersection, where several people have been killed accidentally.

Write a composition of at least 200 words describing how terrible the situation is to your neighbors and stating the reasons why the sign should be installed. Give at least two reasons. Explain each reason.

Diagnosis

MODEL PAPERS

Part I—Business Letter

15 Clinton Street
Brooklyn, NY 11235   Heading
March 19, 1983

Inside address

Supervisor
Carpet Cleaning
15 Rogers Road
Brooklyn, NY 11234

Salutation

Dear Supervisor:

    The repeated calls your telephone solicitor has made to my home have caused a great deal of annoyance as well as interference with my family privacy.

PARAGRAPH 1: The <u>cause</u> of the complaint—repeated calls

    On January 3, we were interrupted with a request to provide a free estimate. This was prime time, at dinner hour. On January 22, another call to offer the same service interrupted our Saturday evening party. Again

PARAGRAPH 2: Details to show the <u>effects</u> of the calls

> on February 11, a third call disturbed my mother's nap. Still a fourth call, on March 10, once more came while we were eating.
>
> All these calls are an invasion of our privacy. I urge you to refrain from this practice.

PARAGRAPH 3: A strong request to refrain from disturbance

> Very truly yours,
>
> May Black

Complimentary close

Signature

Diagnosis

This above business letter of complaint:

1. Responds to the writing purpose.
2. Follows a clear paragraph scheme:

   Paragraph 1: Makes the complaint clear.
   Paragraph 2: Gives details to support that complaint.
   Paragraph 3: Voices a strong request to refrain.

3. Is free of major mechanical errors.
4. Arranges details on a *cause-effect basis*—the cause (frequent business calls at bad times) and the effect (invasion of the family's privacy).

Part II—The Report

> Westminster Abbey, located in the heart of London, <u>is a lovely place to visit.</u> Having reviewed tour books first to learn more about this famous place, I hired a guide to lead me through the many sections on July 4.

Expanded information

Combining two notes

PARAGRAPH 1: Notes on preparation for the visit

> As I entered the main hall, I looked about me and was amazed at the huge size of the abbey. Above me were enormous stained-glass windows, a very high-domed ceiling, and several richly decorated altars. To the left and right were small chapels, icons, and beautifully carved statuary. The most beautiful was one of Jesus summoning Mary to join him on his wanderings, the entire piece enveloped in reddish light.
>
> The visit was so rewarding that I returned on July 9, when I spent a great deal of time studying the crypts of famous people and wandering through a museum of sacred relics.

Added information (highlighted portions)

PARAGRAPH 2: What the visitor sees around him (spatial observations)

PARAGRAPH 3: Notes on the return visit and what the visitor saw

Diagnosis

This report on an interesting place:

1. Includes all the basic notes.
2. Expands on these notes.
3. Adds additional information.
4. Structures three paragraphs:

    Paragraph 1: Preparation for the visit.
    Paragraph 2: Details of what the visitor sees around him (*arranged spatially*).
    Paragraph 3: A return visit to admire other features of the abbey.

5. Is free of major mechanical errors.

Two Model Tests

Part III—Composition

<u>Emphatic statement</u>

How unfortunate that tragic deaths must occur before a community takes action. Here, three people have already lost their lives because of a dangerous intersection that has no "stop" sign.

It is amazing that of all the many children who pass through each day to go to school, none has been injured. Although there is a school guard stationed on the corner of Huston and Bleeker, cars very often ignore her signals.

Considering the many minor mishaps we had already, involving cars hitting one another, it's again amazing that no one was seriously hurt until this year. When you picture four roadways converging without lights or stop signs, the possibilities are frightening.

Mr. Jones was a lovely old man who never saw the car racing at him; nor did Maggie Burns, a mother of three children; nor did John Baxter our minister, who also lost his life unnecessarily. What a terrible waste!

<u>Emphatic question</u>

Community residents, don't you think it's time to demand correction of this intolerable situation?

PARAGRAPH 1: The writer refers to the problem clearly

PARAGRAPH 2: The writer underscores the problem with reference to schoolchildren

PARAGRAPH 3: The writer highlights the problem with reference to heavy traffic

PARAGRAPH 4: The writer offers the most convincing reason—three deaths (ascending order)

Diagnosis

This persuasive composition:

1. States the problem in Paragraph 1.
2. Highlights the problem in Paragraph 2.

213

3. Highlights it further in Paragraph 3.
4. Stresses it most convincingly in Paragraph 4.
5. Uses the *ascending order pattern*—saving the most important reason for last.
6. Concludes forcefully in Paragraph 5.
7. Employs emphatic statements to make the point persuasively.
8. Is free of major mechanical errors.

HOW TO EVALUATE YOUR PROGRESS

After you have studied the section "Diagnosis: Model Papers," you should have a good idea as to what constitutes an acceptable business letter, report, and persuasive composition. The same components used to illustrate good writing in the samples should appear in your own writing.

To judge whether you are indeed making gains, ask yourself these questions after you have completed a particular writing task:

WRITER'S CHECKLIST		
Business Letter	Yes	No
1. Did I explain the problem?		
2. Did I make clear what I want the company to do?		
3. Did I give complete and correct information?		
4. Did I use an acceptable business letter form?		

Report	Yes	No
1. Did I carry out the given task?		
2. Did I use all the notes?		
3. Did I organize the notes in a certain pattern?		
4. Have I used paragraphs to show separation of ideas?		
5. Did I review my paper for proper sentence structure, grammatical correctness, and proper usage?		

Composition	Yes	No
1. Did I address myself to the question?		
2. Did I state a clear position?		
3. Did I support that position with sufficient reasons?		
4. Did I arrange these reasons into a certain pattern?		
5. Did I conclude with a sentence that relates to my opening?		
6. Did I write enough words?		
7. Did I review my paper for proper sentence structure, grammatical correctness, and proper usage?		

GLOSSARY OF GRAMMATICAL TERMS

Adjectival clauses and phrases: Groups of words that contain a subject and a verb used to describe another part of the sentence.
Example: The meeting *which I attended* lasted three hours.

Adverbial clauses: Groups of words that contain a subject and a verb used to show when an action occurs.
Example: *When I returned home*, I found the letter in my mailbox.

Adverbial conjunctions: Words that begin clauses to modify another word.
Example: He sat with me *when* I was in the theater and remained *until* I left.

Appositives: Words added to a sentence to provide explanations but that are not necessary to the basic meaning.
Example: Mr. James Baline, *who is the manager of your store*, spoke with me.

Incident reference words: Words that specifically refer to supportive details.
Example: *One reason* why I am writing is to tell you I am displeased with the product.
Another is to report that the item I purchased was of inferior quality.
A third reason is that it was overpriced.

Parenthetical words: Words that are a part of a sentence but that are not essential to the basic meaning.
Example: It was, *I must admit*, a most unfortunate matter.

Prepositional phrases: Groups of words that begin with a preposition.
Example: *In my house*, I often watch birds *from the window*.

Relative clauses: Groups of words that contain a subject and a verb used to relate a previous part of the sentence.
Example: I went back to the school of my childhood, *where I visited some teachers I knew from before*.

Transitionals: Words that connect sentences to show relationships.
Example: *First*, I emptied my pocket. *Then* I placed my wallet on the table. *Finally*, I counted my change.

APPENDIX—BASIC SKILLS REVIEW

This book has shown you not only how to organize your ideas into effective business letters, reports, and persuasive compositions but also how to use language to convey these ideas correctly. This use of language to convey information clearly and concisely involves certain skills and a knowledge of mechanics.

A command of basic skills is very important in writing. It may mean the difference between passing or failing the Regents Competency Test in Writing. Therefore, let's review the major skills involved in the preceding lesson units.

Skill 1

SENTENCE STRUCTURE

WHAT IS A SIMPLE SENTENCE?

A sentence is a group of words that (1) has a *subject* (one who does something), (2) has a *verb* (an action word), and (3) *expresses a complete thought.*

Examples

1. In the morning, John wakens to go to school.
2. Bill often goes to the movies, spending many hours there.
3. Throwing his book away, Tom went home.

Analysis

Example 1
Subject: John
Verb: wakens
Simple thought: John wakens to go to school.

Example 2
Subject: Bill
Verb: goes
Simple thought: Bill goes to the movies.

Example 3
Subject: Tom
Verb: went
Simple thought: Tom went home.

Appendix—Basic Skills Review

Test (See answers on page 245.)

Directions

Now see whether you understand the elements of a sentence. Identify (1) the subject, (2) the verb, and (3) the simple thought in each of the following sentences.

1. In the afternoon, Jerry strolled around the corner.
   Subject: _____
   Verb: _____
   Simple thought: _____
2. Recognizing his error, Bill made the correction.
   Subject: _____
   Verb: _____
   Simple thought: _____
3. Alice rushed to her class, after being late.
   Subject: _____
   Verb: _____
   Simple thought: _____

Compound Subjects and Verbs

Sometimes a simple sentence can have more than one subject or verb. When two subjects are present, we identify them as a *compound subject*. When two verbs appear, we identify them as a *compound verb*.

Examples of Simple Sentences with Compound Subjects

1. Jerry and his friend Bill went to the game.
2. In the corner sat Alice and Joan.
3. In the morning, the sun and the birds appeared very picturesque.

Analysis

Example 1
Compound subject: Jerry and his friend Bill
Verb: went
Simple thought: Jerry and Bill went to the game.

Example 2
Compound subject: Alice and Joan
Verb: sat
Simple thought: Alice and Joan sat in the corner.

Example 3
Compound subject: the sun and the birds
Verb: seemed
Simple thought: The sun and the birds seemed very picturesque.

Examples of Simple Sentences with Compound Verbs

1. Both parents worried and waited up late for their daughter.
2. After lunch, Jerry ran and romped in the schoolyard.
3. Away from the others, Alice sat and thought all by herself.

Analysis

Example 1
Subject: Both parents
Compound verb: worried and waited up
Simple thought: Both parents worried and waited up.

Example 2
Subject: Jerry
Compound verb: ran and romped
Simple thought: Jerry ran and romped.

Example 3
Subject: Alice
Compound verb: sat and thought
Simple thought: Alice sat and thought.

Test (See answers on page 245.)

Directions

Now see whether you understand both compound subjects and compound verbs by underlining them in the following simple sentences.

1. Benny and his friends jeered and yelled at the opposing players.

Compound subject: _____
Compound verb: _____
2. In the streets, adults and children cheered and supported the new law.
Compound subject: _____
Compound verb: _____
3. Senators and representatives write and read a great deal when the legislature is in session.
Compound subject: _____
Compound verb: _____

REMEMBER: A sentence can have many subjects and verbs. However, if it conveys one main, unifying idea, it is a simple sentence.

THE COMPOUND SENTENCE

A compound sentence has two main ideas joined by a *coordinate conjunction* (connecting word). Each idea can stand by itself as complete . Common coordinate conjunctions are *and, but, or, for, nor*.

Examples of Compound Sentences

1. You wait here, and I'll find out the time.
2. Bill wanted to have friends, but nobody liked him.
3. I like working, but the truth is that it's time-consuming.

Analysis

Example 1
Main idea 1: You wait here
Main idea 2: I'll find out the time
Conjunction: and

Example 2
Main idea 1: Bill wanted to have friends
Main idea 2: nobody liked him
Conjunction: but

Example 3
Main idea 1: I like working
Main idea 2: the truth is it's time consuming
Conjunction: but

Appendix—Basic Skills Review

Test (See answers on page 245.)

Directions

Now see whether you understand the elements of the compound sentence by identifying (1) main idea 1, (2) main idea 2, (3) the connecting word (conjunction).

1. You give me an honest man, and I'll give you a fortune.
   Main idea 1: _____
   Main idea 2: _____
   Conjunction: _____
2. He tempted me with money, but my good sense told me to refuse.
   Main idea 1: _____
   Main idea 2: _____
   Conjunction: _____
3. Everyone knows the truth, but few are willing to speak it.
   Main idea 1: _____
   Main idea 2: _____
   Conjunction: _____

REMEMBER: A compound sentence must have two independent ideas that can stand alone, each as a simple sentence. The conjunction is the bridge that connects them.

THE COMPLEX SENTENCE

A complex sentence is one that has only one main idea (*independent clause*) and one or more dependent ideas (*dependent clauses*).

Examples of Complex Sentences

1. When spring comes, most birds fly north.
2. Alice was irritable because she hadn't slept.
3. Since the team lost, spirit is lower.

Analysis

Example 1
Main idea: most birds fly south
Dependent idea: When spring comes

Example 2
Main idea: Alice was irritable
Dependent idea: because she hadn't slept.

Example 3
Main idea: spirit is lower
Dependent idea: Since the team lost

Further Examples

1. When school opens and when children return to school, parents are happy.
2. Although we knew his name, we didn't say anything.
3. We took vacation because we were tired and because we needed a break.

Analysis

Example 1
Main idea: parents are happy
Dependent idea: When school opens
Dependent idea: when children return to school

Example 2
Main idea: we didn't say anything
Dependent idea: Although we knew his name

Example 3
Main idea: We took a vacation
Dependent idea: because we were tired
Dependent idea: because we needed a break

Test (See answers on page 245.)

Directions

Now see whether you understand the elements of the complex sentence by identifying (1) the main idea and (2) the dependent idea or ideas.

1. Wherever he goes, people always look at him.
   Main idea: _____
   Dependent idea: _____
2. The police arrested him, though he was innocent.
   Main idea: _____
   Dependent idea: _____

3. The family gets together when there is an occasion or when something important happens.
   Main idea: _____
   Dependent idea: _____
   Dependent idea: _____

REMEMBER: A complex sentence always has one main idea and one or more dependent ideas. *Adverbial conjunctions* introduce dependent ideas. The most common adverbial conjunctions are *because, when, since, though, although.*

GENERAL REVIEW (See answers on page 245.)
Directions

You have now learned there are three basic sentences: Simple, Compound, Complex. *Before you go on, test yourself to see whether you really understand each one by identifying the following sentences.*

_____ 1. Because he left me, I was sad.
_____ 2. Since the weather is bad and since I feel sick, I'll remain in bed.
_____ 3. Jerry and his family went to a picnic.
_____ 4. Study hard and the world is yours.
_____ 5. In the summer, Jeremy swims and plays.

COMMON ERRORS IN SENTENCE STRUCTURE

How you structure your sentences is essential to clear meaning. The Regents Competency Test in Writing requires simple, clear sentences. If you do so, your ideas will be understood. If you don't, your ideas will be fuzzy.

Examine the following paragraph.

Example

It happened when I was ten years old, my friends and I went on a trip to Boston. Where there is a lot of history. We were eager to go, so we left early. My friends and I left Monday, my brother joined us a week later. With my sister even later. The trip was a long one, we were exhausted. Too tired to have much fun. Boston is a nice place to visit, you should go there.

Appendix—Basic Skills Review

What is wrong with the paragraph? Why is it so unclear?

Analysis The answer is that the sentences are poorly structured. Some ideas collide (*run-on sentences*), while others are incomplete (*fragments*).

Run-on: It happened when I was ten years old, my friends and I went to Boston.
Correction: It happened when I was ten years old. My friends and I went to Boston.

Run-on: We were eager to go, so we left early.
Correction: Since we were eager to go, we left early.

Run-on: My friends and I left Monday, my brother joined us a week later.
Correction: My friends and I left Monday, while my brother joined us a week later.

Run-on: The trip was a long one, we were exhausted.
Correction: Because the trip was a long one, we were exhausted.

Run-on: Boston is a nice place to visit, you should go there.
Correction: Boston is a nice place to visit. You should go there.

Fragment: Where there is a lot of history.
Correction: The city has a lot of history.

Fragment: With my sister even later.
Correction: My sister came even later.

Fragment: Too tired to have much fun.
Correction: We were too tired to have much fun.

Reconstructed Paragraph

When I was ten years old, my friends and I went on a trip to Boston. The city has a lot of history. Since we were eager to go, we left early. My friends and I left Monday, while my brother joined us later. My sister came even later. Because the trip was a long one, we were exhausted. We were too tired to have much fun. Boston is a nice place to visit. You should go there.

Do you note how much clearer the second paragraph is? Do you see how well structured the sentences are?

The Run-on Sentence

The run-on sentence is confusing because the ideas run together (collide). The best way to correct is to separate them with a period or to use a conjunction to separate them.

Examples

1. School is boring, students don't like to go.
   Correction 1: School is boring. Students don't like to go.
   Correction 2: Because school is boring, students don't like to go.
2. The test was easy, so we all passed.
   Correction 1: The test was easy. We all passed.
   Correction 2: Since the test was easy, we all passed.
3. The party was a success, we all had fun.
   Correction 1: The party was a success. We all had fun.
   Correction 2: Because the party was a success, we all had fun.

Test (See answers on page 245.)

Directions

Now try your hand at the following run-on sentences. Correct each in two ways.

1. The dance was over early, everyone was disappointed.
   Correction 1: _____
   Correction 2: _____
2. He was very funny, so we laughed.
   Correction 1: _____
   Correction 2: _____
3. I love my parents, they are nice to me.
   Correction 1: _____
   Correction 2: _____

The Sentence Fragment

A sentence fragment is a piece of a sentence. Therefore it is an incomplete sentence, an incomplete idea.

Examples

1. Lounging around at home doing nothing.
   Correction 1: I was lounging around at home doing nothing.
   Correction 2: Lounging around at home and doing nothing is a waste.
2. Too angry to get along with others.

Appendix—Basic Skills Review

Correction 1: Some people are too angry to get along with others.
Correction 2: Too angry to get along with others, John never had friends.
3. Walking home at night.
Correction 1: She was walking home at night when the fire started.
Correction 2: Walking home at night, she saw a fire.

Test (See answers on page 245.)

Directions

Now try your hand at the following sentence fragments. Correct each in two ways.

1. Sitting around with my friends in the evening.
   Correction 1: _____
   Correction 2: _____
2. Too tired to get up in the morning.
   Correction 1: _____
   Correction 2: _____
3. Prepared to do his best on the job.
   Correction 1: _____
   Correction 2: _____

REMEMBER: Run-on sentences have ideas colliding, while fragments are pieces of sentences.

Directions

See whether you can identify each of the following errors—run-ons and fragments—and make the necessary corrections.

_____ 1. Jerry is tall, his brother is short.
   Correction: _____
_____ 2. Around the corner from my house.
   Correction: _____
_____ 3. Sitting around the table with my family.
   Correction: _____
_____ 4. Swimming is important, it builds stamina.
   Correction: _____
_____ 5. The wind banging on the shutters.
   Correction: _____

Skill 2

SENTENCE VARIETY

So far, you have learned the three main kinds of sentences and how to structure your own sentences so that your meanings come through clearly.

Another important element of sentences is interest. Creating variety in sentences helps the reader not only to follow your ideas, but also to be eager to read further. That is what sentence variety achieves.

Here is a paragraph a student wrote. The teacher judged the sentences as uninteresting. Can you see why?

Example

Every evening I sit with my family at dinner. My mother cooks. My father sets the table. We children straighten up after. We sit down to eat together. We talk about what happened during the day. My brother and I tell about school. Mother serves the dishes and then sits down. My dog Shag leaps on our knees for food handouts. I feed her once in awhile. But my father scolds me for spoiling her. My mother tries to make peace. Eating with my family can be fun. It is painful too.

Analysis The above paragraph, though focused on the family together in the evening, is flat and uninspiring because the sentences are:

1. Short and choppy.
2. Unimaginative.
3. Unconnected and therefore not smooth.
4. Lacking in descriptive power.
5. Unrevealing of why the people act as they do.

Reconstructed Paragraph

Now note the improvement in the same situation when the sentences are changed to have more variety.

> *Every evening I sit with my family at dinner, eager to share with them. My mother, who loves to prepare meals, does the cooking, while my father helps set the table; and we children gladly straighten up after. Though we may be busy elsewhere, it is a tradition in our family to sit down together. During the meal, we talk about what happened during the day. My brother and I tell about school, the focus of our day. After this, Mother serves the dishes and sits down. Often, my dog Shag leaps on our knees for food handouts. Since I love her, I feed her once in awhile, but my father scolds me for spoiling her. When this happens, my mother tries to make peace. Eating with my family can be fun, but it can be painful, too.*

Analysis The improved paragraph is more interesting because it contains:

1. Added information.
   - eager to share with them
   - who loves to prepare meals
   - Though we may be busy elsewhere
2. Transitions.
   - During the meal
   - Often
   - When this happens
3. Sentence variety.
   - *Simple sentence*
     During the meal, we talk about what happened during the day.
   - *Complex sentence*
     Since I love her, I feed her once in awhile.
   - *Compound sentence*
     Eating with my family can be fun, but it can be painful, too.

WAYS TO CORRECT SENTENCES THAT LACK VARIETY

1. If your sentences are short and choppy, think of ways of connecting them.
   Example: I love movies. They're exciting.
   Correction: *I love movies because they're exciting.*
2. If your sentences are unimaginative, think of ways of lengthening them.
   Example: Christmas is a great holiday. My family gets together. We have fun.
   Correction: Christmas is a great holiday when my family gets together and we have fun.
3. If your sentences lack descriptive power, then look for ways to add *adjective clauses*. Adjective conjunctions, such as *who, whom, which, that* are common connectives for adjective clauses.
   Example: My mother is the neatest person I have ever seen. Her clothes are always stylish.
   Correction: My mother, who is always conscious of her appearance, is the neatest person I have ever seen. Her clothes, carefully chosen and suited to her looks, are always stylish.
4. If your sentences do not follow smoothly, then you should look for ways of connecting them so that they have a relationship.
   Example: The city scares me. There is so much crime. I hate going there.
   Correction: The city scares me because there is so much crime. Therefore, I hate going there.
5. If your sentences do not reveal *how* people act, then you should try to include adverbs.
   Example: Every time I come home late, my father gets up from bed to greet me. As I enter the house, he comes downstairs and talks with me.
   Correction: Every time I come home late, my father gets up from bed to greet me *angrily*. As I enter the house *quietly so as not to be noticed*, he comes down and scolds me *endlessly*.

REMEMBER: Make an effort to avoid writing sentences that are (1) short and choppy, (2) unimaginative, (3) unconnected, (4) unrevealing, and (5) non-descriptive. Look for ways of writing sentences that interest and engage the reader.

Test (See answers on page 246.)

Directions

Now see whether you can put the above to use, by improving the following sentences.

1. I love dogs. They are good friends.
2. I go to the library. I borrow books. I return them a week later.
3. I go to sleep at night and get up in the morning.
4. My French teacher is a nice person. He is good to me.
5. I have a nice family. Some of my friends do not.

Skill 3

GRAMMAR AND SYNTAX

Writing requires a knowledge of rules that helps to make your ideas clear and precise. Following these rules will enable you to convince your reader that what you are saying is important.

The following pages contain errors that are commonly found in student writing. These errors have been corrected, and rules have been provided to guide you in your own writing.

AGREEMENT

Examples

I discovered one of my checks *were* lost. I now know everyone should secure *their* personal effects. Each item *have* importance.

Analysis   In each sentence, the verb or pronoun does not agree with the subject. The italicized word indicates the specific error.

Correction

I discovered one of my checks *was* lost. I now know everyone should secure *his or her* personal effects. Each item *has* importance.

Rule

Verbs and pronouns must agree with their subjects, or antecedents, in person and number.

PARALLEL STRUCTURE

Examples

I would like to order stamps, an album, and *would like to know where to read about countries*. To have this information, to learn about other lands, and *being able to locate them would be helpful*.

Analysis Neither italicized part is parallel to its previous segments.

Correction

I would like to order stamps, an album, and *a directory of countries*. To have this information, to learn about other lands, and *to be able to locate them would be helpful*.

Rule

Parallel structure refers to the practice of making a series of words, phrases, or clauses consistent with one another.

AWKWARD STRUCTURE

Standard English requires that we write clearly and concisely. Awkward expressions cloud meaning and create a weak effect.

Examples

In the brochure it says the city is an old one. I wanted to know more about *it, so* I read it.

Analysis Each of the two ideas is neither clear nor concise. The italicized parts indicate the awkwardness of expression.

Correction

The brochure says the city is an old one. Since I wanted to know more about it, I read it.

Rule

Express your ideas in as few words as possible. Be clear and concise.

Skill 4

PUNCTUATION

THE COMMA

The comma is an important punctuation mark that has many uses. It helps to make meanings clear. Knowing how to use it will enable you to convey your ideas more effectively.

Examples

Jerry who is my best friend saw the accident. He observed two cars one truck and a van collide. After the accident he reported the details of course. He said it took place at 16 Houston Street New York N.Y.

Analysis   In the sentences above, the meaning is not very clear because commas are omitted. Note how the use of commas improves the sentences.

Correction

Jerry, who is my best friend, saw the accident. He observed two cars, one truck, and a van collide. After the accident, he reported the details, of course. He said it took place at 16 Houston Street, New York, N.Y.

Rule

Commas are used (1) after each item in a series, (2) before and after appositives, (3) after a beginning prepositional phrase, and (4) between the street, city, and state in an address.

Appendix—Basic Skills Review

THE SEMICOLON

The semicolon has one important purpose: to bridge two sentences that are closely related.

Examples

I have to make a report for social studies, it is very important. I was in a car accident, it was terrible.

Analysis The sentences above are closely related, and therefore need the semicolon to show that relationship. The underlined parts are where the semicolons should be placed.

Correction

I have to make a report for social studies; it is very important. I was in a car accident; it was terrible.

Rule

The semicolon joins two sentences that are very close in meaning.

THE COLON

The colon has two important uses. These uses will enable you to express your ideas more effectively.

Examples

Dear Sir

    I need information on two events you held a parade and a circus.

Analysis The salutation "Dear Sir" is not appropriately written. The sentence, because it does not have a colon, appears to be a run-on.

Correction

Dear Sir:

    I need information on two events you held: a parade and a circus.

Rule

The colon is used after a salutation in a business letter and after a particular word that needs further explanation.

THE APOSTROPHE

The apostrophe is another important punctuation mark that has two uses: to show possession and to contract two separate words into one.

Examples

My schools cutting policy is different from John Jays. Its too bad youre not a student here.

Analysis   Because of the omission of apostrophes, it is not clear whether the cutting policy applies to one or more schools. Also, the possessive pronouns do not indicate the letters that were omitted.

Correction

My school's cutting policy is different from John Jay's. It's too bad you're not a student here.

Rule

The apostrophe shows (1) possession and (2) a contraction that omits one or more letters.

QUOTATION MARKS

Quotation marks are commonly used to set off the actual words a speaker uses, as well as to punctuate titles.

Examples

I heard the speaker say all of you must help us. He asked that we read a story called A War of Nerves.

Analysis   Quotations marks are needed to (1) set off the words spoken and (2) to punctuate the title of the story.

Correction

I heard the speaker say, "All of you must help us." He asked that we read a story called "A War of Nerves."

Rule

Quotation marks are used to show those words that a speaker *actually* uses and to highlight titles of stories and chapters.

Skill 5

CAPITALIZATION

Capitals are used, of course, to begin sentences, but they are also used for specific persons, places, and things.

Examples

I visited the white house in washington, d.c. for my history report. While there, I bought two goodyear tires at a shell station. After, we drove to valley forge to study george washington's role in the american revolution. Next year, I plan to take health ed, american history, science, and spanish.

Analysis The above paragraph contains reference to specific persons, places, and things. These items require capital letters.

Correction

I visited the White House in Washington, D.C. for my history report. While there, I bought two Goodyear tires at a Shell station. After, we drove to Valley Forge to study George Washington's role in the American Revolution. Next year, I plan to take health ed, American history, science, and Spanish.

Rule

Words are capitalized when they refer to specific persons, places, and things.

Skill 6

SPELLING AND USAGE

Our language has a number of words that sound alike but are spelled differently. Since they cause a great deal of difficulty, it is important to learn how to distinguish both the spelling and the meaning. The following are common pairs of words that will be useful in your writing.

ACCEPT, EXCEPT

Examples

I cannot *accept* the shipment *except* for a few items.

Analysis   If I *accept* the shipment, I will take it. *Except* for a few items means that I am excluding most of the shipment.

Rule

Accept: to take or receive.
Except: excluding or without.

AFFECT, EFFECT

Example

A poor grade can *affect* your class performance, and the *effect* on your final average can be considerable.

Analysis The use of *affect* expresses the idea of causing a change, while the word *effect* refers to the consequence of doing poorly.

Rule

Affect: a verb that means "to change or influence."
Effect: a noun that means "the result or consequence."

ALREADY, ALL READY

Examples

Now that we have *already* interviewed the speaker, we are *all ready* to go.

Analysis *Already* interviewed shows that the interview is completed. if we are *all ready* to go, we are prepared to make the departure.

Rule

Already: just, previously.
All ready: prepared to do something.

ALRIGHT, ALL RIGHT

Examples

All right, you may join us when you are feeling *all right*.

Analysis *Alright* is not acceptable as proper usage.

Rule

All right: an adverb used to emphasize a point or to express a condition of feeling fine.

ALTOGETHER, ALL TOGETHER

Example

We gathered in the room, *all together*. *Altogether*, there were ten people assembled.

Analysis The word *all together* shows people assembling. The word *altogether* indicates the total number.

Rule

All together: a group in one place for a reason.
Altogether: completely, entirely.

FORMALLY, FORMERLY

Examples

I dressed *formally* for the occasion because I *formerly* was a member of the group.

Analysis To dress *formally* is to put on your best clothes, while *formerly* being a member shows that you once belonged.

Rule

Formally: exactly, traditionally.
Formerly: at one time, before.

IT'S, ITS

It's too bad you weren't there when the dog wagged *its* tail.

Analysis The first *it's* combines "it is" and the second *its* shows that the tail belongs to the dog.

Rule

It's: a contraction for "it is."
Its: a possessive adjective showing ownership.

LOAN, LEND

Examples

I visited the bank to *loan* money and went to my friend's house to *lend* a book.

Analysis The word *loan* refers to money you borrow for a period of time, while *lend* may refer to any other item you borrow for a period of time.

Rule

Loan: borrow money.
Lend: borrow anything but money.

PERSONAL, PERSONNEL

Examples

Report to the *personnel* office where you will be asked to give *personal* information.

Analysis A *personnel* office is where you are interviewed for a job, while *personal* information consists of details about your own life.

Rule

Personnel: a staff of workers or an office.
Personal: private, information about yourself.

PRINCIPAL, PRINCIPLE

Example

My *principal* reason for seeing him was that I was upset. I spoke with Mr. Katz, the *principal* of the school. We spoke about the *principles* of learning.

Analysis My *principal* reason would be my most important reason, while the *principal* of the school would be the most important person. The *principles* of learning would be the ways in which we learn.

Rule

Principal: the main or most important reason or person.
Principle: a concept or idea.

STATIONARY, STATIONERY

Examples

I placed my box of *stationery* on my *stationary* desk.

Analysis *Stationery* is a word that applies to anything belonging in an office, such as envelopes and stamps, while a *stationary* desk is a desk that is not movable.

Rule

Stationery: writing material.
Stationary: not moving, in one place.

THERE, THEIR, THEY'RE

Example

There are three things you must do. One is to put your coat over *there*. Another is to join your friends at *their* house. A third is to talk to them because *they're* the type of people you admire.

Analysis *There* specifies what has to be done, as well as a place. The combination *their* house shows that the house belongs to friends. The word *they're* represents "they are."

Rule

There: an adverb that designates a place.
Their: a possessive adjective.
They're: a contraction for "they are."

TO, TOO

Example

Because I was *too* upset, I went *to* sleep. I will be rested, *too*.

Analysis *Too* upset shows a condition of being *very* upset. *To* sleep indicates a direction taken, while the use of *too* shows that I will be rested, as well.

Rule

To: a preposition indicating a direction.
Too: an adverb meaning very or as well.

YOU'RE, YOUR

Example

You're the first one I respect. I concede to *your* point of view.

Analysis The contraction *you're* consists of "you are," while *your* point of view expresses a point of view that belongs to you.

Rule

You're: a contraction for "you are."
Your: a possessive adjective that shows ownership.

WE'RE, WERE, WHERE

Examples

We're the family that bought that radio when you *were* there, but we don't know *where* our receipt is.

Analysis *We're* the family really means "We are the family." The verb *were* shows a state of being, while *where* is an adverb showing place.

Rule

We're: a contraction for "we are."
Were: a verb that shows a state of being.
Where: an adverb designating a place.

Answers

What Is a Simple Sentence?/Test   Page 219

1. Subject: Jerry
   Verb: strolled
   Simple thought: Jerry strolled around the corner.

2. Subject: Bill
   Verb: made
   Simple thought: Bill made the correction.

3. Subject: Alice
   Verb: rushed
   Simple thought: Alice rushed to her class,

Compound Subjects and Verbs/Test   Page 220

1. Compound subject: Benny and his friends
   Compound verb: jeered and yelled

2. Compound subject: adults and children
   Compound verb: cheered and supported

3. Compound subject: Senators and representatives
   Compound verb: write and read

The Compound Sentence/Test   Page 222

1. Main idea 1: You give me an honest man,
   Main idea 2: I'll give you a fortune.
   Conjunction: and

2. Main idea 1: He tempted me with money,
   Main idea 2: my good sense told me to refuse.
   Conjunction: but

3. Main idea 1: Everyone knows the truth,
   Main idea 2: few are willing to speak it.
   Conjunction: but

The Complex Sentence/Test   Page 223

1. Main idea: people always look at him.
   Dependent idea: Wherever he goes,

2. Main idea: The police arrested him,
   Dependent idea: though he was innocent.

3. Main idea: The family gets together
   Dependent idea: when there is an occasion
   Dependent idea: when something important happens.

General Review   Page 224

1. Complex
2. Complex
3. Simple
4. Compound
5. Simple

The Run-on Sentence/Test   Page 226

1. Correction 1: The dance was over early. Everyone was disappointed.
   Correction 2: Because the dance was over early, everyone was disappointed.

2. Correction 1: He was very funny. We laughed.
   Correction 2: Since he was very funny, we laughed.

3. Correction 1: I love my parents. They are nice to me.
   Correction 2: I love my parents because they are nice to me.

The Sentence Fragment/Test   Page 227

1. Correction 1: I was sitting around with my friends in the evening.
   Correction 2: Sitting around with my friends in the evening, I had a good time.

2. Correction 1: She was too tired to get up in the morning.
   Correction 2: Too tired to get up in the morning, she stayed in bed.

3. Correction 1: He was prepared to do his best on the job.
   Correction 2: Prepared to do his best on the job, Henry went to work.

---

1. Correction: Run-on—Jerry is tall, but his brother is short.
2. Correction: Fragment—The police station is around the corner from my house.
3. Correction: Fragment—Sitting around the table with my family, I told several jokes.
4. Correction: Run-on—Swimming is important because it builds stamina.
5. Correction: Fragment—Jane was distracted by the wind banging on the shutters.

Sentence Variety/Test   Page 231

1. Dogs are acknowledged to be man's best friend, and it is easy to see why I love them.
2. I have gotten into the habit of borrowing books from the library and returning them a week later.
3. I go to sleep reluctantly at night and get up unwillingly in the morning.
4. My French teacher, a warm and caring person, has been extremely helpful to me.
5. Although I am fortunate enough to have a marvelous family, some of my friends do not.

Appendix

Answers for Chapter 3

Pattern 1: Chronological Order/Test   Page 27

The meeting started early and ended early. The first speaker was an ex-offender who spoke about his life. Our second speaker at the Youth Rehabilitation Center asked for our support. The last item on the agenda was the matter of volunteering time. Before that, there was plea by the treasurer for dues payment.

Pattern 2: Ascending Order/Test   Page 30

One important reason is that it's a hardship to wait and wait. Another important reason is that your agent already checked the damage and filed the claim. The most important reason is that I can't fix the car till I receive a settlement.

Pattern 3: Descending Order/Test   Page 31

Above all, a father should be very understanding and sympathetic. A father should take an interest in his children. It's also important for a father to play with his children.

Pattern 4: Cause and Effect/Test   Page 32

Frequent break-ins in schools—*cause*
There is a lot of damage to windows—*effect*

Students are usually the perpetrators—*cause*
They show their disregard for property—*effect*

Custodians have to deal with intruders—*cause*
Other maintenance is being ignored—*effect*

Costs of repairs are high—*cause*
The taxpayers bear the burden of loss—*effect*

There have been frequent break-ins in schools, causing a lot of damage to windows. Students, usually the perpetrators, have been showing their disregard for property. Custodians have to deal with the intruders, while other maintenance is ignored. And when costs of repairs are high, the taxpayers bear the burden of loss.

Pattern 5: Spatial Order/Test   Page 33–34

Noisy, busy stream of people
Long aisles that lead to food sections
A variety of aromas that permeates the store
Food shelves stocked plentifully
Cashiers busily ringing registers

The supermarket at which we shop is a lively store with a hectic atmosphere. During the day it is filled with a noisy, busy stream of people. Long aisles lead to the food sections, and a variety of aromas permeates the store. Although the food shelves are stocked plentifully, they need to be replenished regularly, as the cashiers are busily ringing their registers throughout the day.

Pattern 6: Comparison and Contrast/Test   Page 35

	Friend 1	Friend 2
	Detail 1: tall	Detail 1: short
	Detail 2: shy	Detail 2: outgoing
	Detail 3: serious	Detail 3: comical

Most people find it amusing that I can be close friends with two people who are as different as Hal and Eddie. Hal is the center on our school's basketball team and is quite tall, while Eddie is only 5 feet tall. In terms of their personalities, Hal is shy and withdrawn but Eddie is breezy, outgoing, and friendly. Eddie likes to joke around and make me laugh; on the other hand, Hal is serious and thoughtful.

INDEX

Adding of details/words, 101, 136, 193
Address. *See* Inside address
Adjectival clauses, 115, 118, 245
Adverbial clauses, 58, 66, 110, 115, 118, 153, 245
Adverbial conjunctions, 245
Agreement, 232
Answers
  ascending order, 28–29
  cause and effect, 31–32
  chronological order, 26–27
  comparison/contrast, 34–35
  descending order, 30–31
  diagnostic test, 14–25
  model papers, 201–207, 210–214
  sample from RCT, 9–11
  spatial order, 33
  See also Models
Apostrophe, 236
Appositives, 109, 245
Arrangement. *See* Organization of ideas/details
Ascending order of ideas/details, 5, 28–30
  for business letter of complaint, 38, 43, 47
  for composition, persuasive, 146, 149, 152, 156, 160
  for report based on information given, 89, 92, 97
Awkward structure, 233

Basic skills, 217–244
Business letter of complaint, 1, 4, 36–37
  checklist, 38
  diagnostic test
    answers, 14–17
    exercises, 12
  about inferior product, 65–68
  about inflated bill, 73–75
  about lost baggage, 53–56
  about lost order, 57–60
  about misleading advertisement, 61–64
  model, 37–38
  model tests
    answers, 201–202, 210–211
    exercises, 198, 208
  outlines of problem situations, 39–40
  RCT
    answers, 9–10
    exercises, 7
  about restaurant incident, 69–72
  about school regulation, 49–52
  about teacher's attitude, 80–83
  about theater ticket mix-up, 45–48
  thinking through problem situations, 39
  about undeserved traffic ticket, 41–44
  about unreceived payment, 76–79
  about unsatisfactory travel experience, 84–87

Capitalization, 238
Cause and effect organization of ideas/details, 5–6, 31–32
  for business letter of complaint, 38, 82, 87
  for composition, persuasive, 146, 176, 180
  for report based on information given, 89, 124

Checklists
  business letter of complaint, 38
  composition, persuasive, 145–146
  report based on information given, 89
Chronological order of ideas/details, 4, 26–28
  for business letter of complaint, 38, 59, 63, 67, 71, 75, 78
  for composition, persuasive, 145, 185
  for report based on information given, 89, 106, 109, 115, 118
Clauses
  adjectival, 115, 118, 245
  adverbial, 58, 66, 110, 115, 118, 153, 245
  dependent, 222
  independent, 222
  relative, 119, 246
Coherence of ideas/details, 2, 26
Colon, 235–236
Combining of notes, 97, 101, 123, 133, 140
Comma, 234
Comparison of ideas/details, 6, 34–35
  in composition, persuasive, 146, 192
  in report based on information given, 89, 127
Comparative words/phrases, 128
Complaint letter. *See* Business letter of complaint
Complete thoughts, 218
Complex sentences, 46, 77, 110, 153, 157, 160, 172, 181, 222–224
Complimentary close of letter, 38, 42, 47, 51, 54, 59, 63, 67, 71, 74, 78, 81, 86
Composition, persuasive, 1, 4, 144
  checklist, 145–146
  diagnostic test
    answers, 22–25
    exercises, 14
  to legislator about increased school funds, 187–191
  to local police about more frequent patrols, 179–182
  to local public official about more jobs, 159–162
  model, 145
  model tests
    answers, 204–205, 213–214
    exercises, 199–200, 209
  to parents about helping finance car, 192–196
  to readers of school paper about petition, 171–174
  to readers of school paper about school money, 155–158
  RCT
    answers, 11
    exercises, 8
  to school board about completing project, 183–186
  to school principal about dropping subject, 147–150
  to school principal about smoking room, 167–170
  to teacher about changing mark, 151–154
  to television station about upgrading quality, 175–178
  thinking through position and reasons, 146

  to town council about improving service, 163–166
Compound sentences, 77, 157, 221–222
Compound subjects, 219
Compound verbs, 219
Comprehensive Regents Test in English, 3
Concluding paragraphs, 2, 4, 38–39, 42, 47, 51, 54, 59, 63, 67, 71, 74, 78, 81, 86, 93, 97, 102, 106, 110, 115, 119, 123, 128, 133, 137, 141, 149, 153, 157, 161, 165, 169, 173, 177, 181, 185, 189–190, 194
  See also Paragraphs
Conjunctions
  adverbial, 245
  coordinate, 221
Contrast of ideas/details, 6, 34–35
  in composition, persuasive, 146, 188
  in report based on information given, 89, 132
Contrasting words/phrases, 133, 189
Coordinate conjunctions, 221
Criteria, general, for RCT, 2

Dependent clauses, 222
Descending order of ideas/details, 4–5, 30–31
  for business letter of complaint, 38, 51, 55
  for composition, persuasive, 146, 165, 168, 173
  for report based on information given, 89, 101
Development of ideas, 2, 4
Diagnostic test, 12–25
  business letter of complaint
    answers, 14–17
    exercises, 12
  composition, persuasive
    answers, 22–25
    exercises, 14
  report based on information given
    answers, 17–21
    exercises, 13
Direct quotations, 42
Directions for RCT, 3–4
Drafting (writing), 1, 3–4

Editing (revising), 1, 4
Examples. *See* Answers
Exercises
  ascending order, 30
  cause and effect, 32
  chronological order, 27–28
  comparison/contrast, 35
  descending order, 31
  diagnostic test, 12–14
  model tests, 197–200, 208–209
  sample from RCT, 7–8
  spatial order, 33–34
Expanding of notes, 97, 123, 140–141

Fleshing out reasons, 164
Fragments, sentence, 226

Grammar, 232–233, 245–246
Guidelines, general, for RCT, 2

Heading of letter, 37, 42, 46, 50, 54, 58, 62, 66, 70, 74, 77, 81, 85
Holistic rating method of RCT, 2

Incident reference words, 81, 245–246

Index

Independent clauses, 222
Informative report. *See* Report based on information given
Inside address of letter, 37, 42, 46, 50, 54, 58, 62, 66, 70, 74, 77, 81, 85
Introductory paragraphs, 2, 4, 37, 39, 42, 46, 50, 54, 58, 62, 66, 70, 74, 77, 81, 85, 92, 97, 101, 106, 109, 115, 118, 123, 128, 133, 137, 140, 148, 152, 156, 160, 164, 168, 172, 176, 180, 184, 189, 193
See also Paragraphs

Letter, business. *See* Business letter of complaint
Logic of ideas/details, 2, 26

Model papers, 201–207, 210–214
Model tests, 197–200, 208–209
Models
  business letter of complaint, 37–38, 42, 46–47, 50–51, 54, 58–59, 62–63, 66–67, 70–71, 74, 77–78, 81, 85–86
  composition, persuasive, 145, 148–149, 152–153, 156–157, 160–161, 164–165, 168–169, 172–173, 176–177, 180–181, 184–185, 189–190, 193–194
  report based on information given, 92–93, 97, 101–102, 106, 109–110, 118–119, 123, 128, 133, 137, 140–141
See also Answers

Name in letter, 38, 42, 47, 51, 54, 59, 63, 67, 71, 74, 78, 81, 86
Notes
  combining of, 97, 101, 123, 133, 140
  expanding of, 97, 123, 140–141

Organization of ideas/details, 4–7, 26–35
  ascending order, 5, 28–30, 38, 43, 47, 89, 92, 97, 146, 149, 152, 156, 160
  cause and effect, 5–6, 31–32, 38, 82, 87, 89, 124, 146, 176, 180
  chronological order, 4, 26–28, 38, 59, 63, 67, 71, 75, 78, 89, 106, 115, 118, 145, 185
  comparison/contrast, 6, 34–35, 89, 127, 132, 146, 188, 192
  descending order, 4–5, 30–31, 38, 51, 55, 89, 101, 146, 165, 168, 173
  spatial order, 6–7, 33–34, 89, 136, 140
Outlines
  for business letter of complaint, 39–40
  for composition, persuasive, 146, 148, 151–152, 156, 160, 164, 168, 172, 176, 180, 184, 188, 192–193
  preliminary, 3
  refined, 3–4
  for report based on information given, 89–90
Paragraphs
  in business letter of complaint, 37–39, 42, 46–47, 50–51, 54, 58–59, 62–63, 66–67, 70–71, 74, 77–78, 81, 85–86

  in composition, persuasive, 148–149, 152–153, 156–157, 160–161, 164–165, 168–169, 172–173, 176–177, 180–181, 184–185, 189–190, 193–194
  in report based on information given, 92–93, 97, 101–102, 106, 109–110, 115, 118–119, 123, 128, 133, 137, 140–141
  used for separate ideas, 2
  See also Concluding paragraphs; Introductory paragraphs
Parallel structure, 233
Parenthetical expressions, 123, 168–169, 173, 246
Persuasive composition. *See* Composition, persuasive
Planning, 1, 3
  See also Outlines
Preliminary outlines, 3
Preliminary Regents Competency Test (PCT) in Writing, 2
Prepositional phrases, 58, 66, 110, 115, 119, 157, 246
Progress evaluations, 206–207, 215–216
Punctuation, 234–237
Purpose, statement of, 2, 4
  See also Introductory paragraphs

Questions. *See* Exercises
Quotation marks, 236–237
Quotations, direct, 42

RCT in Writing. *See* Regents Competency Test in Writing
Refined outlines, 3–4
Regents Competency Test (RCT) in Writing
  general guidelines, 2
  importance, 3
  model papers, 197, 201–205, 210–214
    business letter of complaint, 201–202, 210–211
    composition, persuasive, 204–205, 213–214
    report based on information given, 202–203, 211–212
  model tests, 197–200, 208–209
    business letter of complaint, 198, 208
    composition, persuasive, 199–200, 209
    report based on information given, 199, 209
  organization of ideas/details, 4–7
    ascending order, 5
    cause and effect, 5–6
    chronological order, 4
    comparison/contrast, 6
    descending order, 4–5
    spatial order, 6–7
  rating method, 2
  sample answers, 9–11
    business letter of complaint, 9–10
    composition, persuasive, 11
    report based on information given, 10
  sample exercises, 7–8
    business letter of complaint, 7
    composition, persuasive, 8
    report based on information given, 8

  useful hints, 3–4
  uses, 3
  what is it, 1
  who takes it, 2–3
Relative clauses, 119, 246
Report based on information given, 1, 4, 88, 143
  on athletic event in another school, 126–130
  checklist, 89
  diagnostic test
    answers, 17–21
    exercises, 13
  on live television program, 135–138
  on local hospital conditions, 121–125
  model tests
    answers, 202–203, 211–212
    exercises, 199, 209
  on nature-study trip, 139–142
  on prom at friend's school, 131–134
  on rally against draft, 100–103
  RCT
    answers, 10
    exercises, 8
  on school board meeting, 113–116
  on school event, 108–112
  on school principal interview, 95–99
  on student organization meeting, 104–107
  on talk by ex-student, 91–94
  thinking through report situations, 89–90
  on trip, 117–120
Revising (editing), 1, 4
Run-on sentences, 225

Salutation of letter, 37, 42, 46, 50, 54, 58, 62, 66, 70, 74, 77, 81, 85
Sample answers, 9–11
Sample exercises, 7–8
Semicolon, 161, 235
Signature in letter, 38, 42, 47, 51, 54, 59, 63, 67, 71, 74, 78, 81, 86
Sentences
  complex, 46, 77, 110, 153, 157, 160, 172, 181, 222–224
  compound, 77, 157, 221–222
  construction of, 2
  fragments, 226
  run-on, 225
  simple, 77, 152, 160, 218–221
  variety, 118, 148–149, 228–231
Simple sentences, 77, 152, 160, 218–221
Spatial order of ideas/details, 6–7, 33–34
  for report based on information given, 89, 136, 140
Spelling, 239–244
Statement of purpose, 2, 4
  See also Introductory paragraphs
Subjects, 218–219
Syntax, 232–233

Tests. *See* Diagnostic test; Exercises; Model tests; Regents Competency Test